The Trouble with
Confucianism

Wm. Theodore de Bary

The Trouble with Confucianism

Harvard University Press
Cambridge, Massachusetts
London, England
1991

Some of the material in Chapters 1, 3, 4, and 6 originally appeared in
the *Tanner Lectures on Human Values,* vol. 10, reprinted by permission
of the University of Utah Press.

This book is printed on acid-free paper, and its binding materials
have been chosen for strength and durability.

Library of Congress Cataloging-in-Publication Data

De Bary, William Theodore, 1919–
    The trouble with Confucianism / Wm. Theodore De Bary.
        p. cm.
    "Some of the material in chapters 1, 3, 4, and 6 originally
appeared in the Tanner lectures on human values, vol. 10"—T.p.
verso.
    Includes bibliographical references and index.
    ISBN 0–674–91015–X (alk. paper)
        1. Confucianism.   2. Neo-Confucianism.   I. Title.
BL1852.D43 1991   91–13249
181'.112—dc20   CIP

To Jacques Barzun

Contents

Preface

NOT LONG AGO it would have seemed almost unthinkable to ask, "What significance has Confucianism for the world today?" Twenty or thirty years ago Confucianism was a dead subject in East Asia for all but a few scholars who could easily be written off as antiquarians. Virtually off-limits to any kind of serious study in Mao's China, Confucianism survived elsewhere, it was often said, only as a museum piece. Indeed, so neglected had Confucius become in China by the time of the Cultural Revolution, and so shadowy a figure was he in most people's minds, that the Gang of Four at the start of their anti-Confucian campaign found him a poor target of attack. Confucius had first to be resurrected before he could be pilloried and crucified. Yet, ever since, he has continued to haunt the scene. Like Harry in Alfred Hitchcock's *The Trouble with Harry*, Confucius has refused to stay buried.

Today too, despite the new, more considered attention given to Confucius, his place is still unsettled and his status unclear. For some younger people, the bitter disillusionment that followed the Cultural Revolution and the eclipse of Mao has left them looking everywhere, abroad and at home, for something to replace the god that failed. For others, heirs of the May Fourth movement and steeped in the anti-Confucian satires of Lu Hsun as they never were in the Confucian classics, Confucianism still lurks as the spectre of a reactionary and repressive past, surviving in antidemocratic, "feudal" features of the current regime. The suspicion, among those who, forty years after "liberation," still seek to be liberated, is that the new pragmatic policy in Beijing gives tacit support to the revival of a conservative ideology that would dampen dissent and buttress the status quo. Even the West's new-found interest in Confucianism is, from this point of view, apt to be dismissed as hopelessly anachronistic. Indeed, for those still disposed to consider religions (perhaps now along with Marxism) as the opiate of the people, any sympathetic approach to Confucianism in the West seems to be a romantic illusion, a wishful idealization of China's past on a par with other pipe dreams of Westerners seeking some escape into Oriental mysticism, Zen Buddhism, or transcendental meditation.

Nor are such divergent views found only in post-Mao China. Similar questions are asked and the same doubts expressed in much of "post-Confucian" East Asia. In Singapore Lee Kuan-yew, the aging leader of probably the most spectacular effort at rapid industrialization in Asia, fears the corrupting effects of a permissive, secular liberalism on the traditional Confucian values and social discipline he considers essential ingredients of Singapore's success. Young Singaporeans, however, hold deep reservations about Lee's authoritarian ways and fear any revival of Confucianism as a prelude to further political repression.

Likewise in Korea, regimes widely viewed as no less authoritarian than Lee's have seemed to promote Confucianism as a conservative force, while students and many intellectuals remain distrustful of it (to such an extent that even an official publication of the Korean Academy of Sciences, *An Introduction to Korean Studies,* reflects a critical view of Confucianism among many modern scholars and discounts its contributions to Korea's historical development). In Taiwan, even though more serious attention is paid to Confucianism as integral to China's cultural heritage, young people do not always share the same loyalties and often seem content simply to ignore it. Meanwhile in Japan Confucianism is widely believed to have played a profound, though subtle, role in Japan's rise to a dominant position in the world economy; yet in Ronald Dore's book *Taking Japan Seriously: A Confucian Perspective on Leading Economic Issues* (Stanford University Press, 1987), readers so far unpersuaded of it will have difficulty identifying in traditional terms what is specifically Confucian in the attitudes Dore describes among the Japanese.

In these circumstances it is a good sign that the official line in the People's Republic today speaks of "seeking truth through facts," ? by looking into what is both "good and bad" in Confucianism. Indeed, only a broad and open-minded approach to the subject will do. Yet if I still have difficulty with the question "What does Confucianism have to offer today?"—often put to me in the places just mentioned—my reaction is not simply the disinclination of the typical academician, or supposedly "disinterested scholar," to commit himself. Without abjuring all value judgments I am still obliged to ask: "Whose Confucianism are we talking about?" If it is the original teachings of Confucius in the *Analects,* then almost nothing said about Confucianism today speaks to that. Indeed even the anti-Confucian diatribes earlier in this century spoke rarely to Confucius' own views but only to later adaptations or distortions of them. If, however, it is not only to the teachings of Confucius, but to those of the other classic thinkers (say, Mencius and Hsün-Tzu) that reference is made, then even assuming one can identify the common denominator among these classical Confucians, on what ground do we stop there, disallowing the testimony of still later thinkers like Chu Hsi and Wang Yang-ming who have made major contributions to the development and amplification of the teaching? What purpose is served by freezing the definition at some moment far in the past, when what we want to know is something about the role of Confucianism yesterday or today? Again, since the question, as we have it, is one raised all over East and Southeast Asia, the answer could take many forms: Korean, Japanese, and Vietnamese, as well as Chinese. Strictly speaking, we would need to consider in each such case how Confucianism was understood and practiced—how it came to be transmitted, interpreted, accepted, and acted upon in this time and that place.

If in the face of such complications, I venture some broad answers to these questions, it is with the hope that the reader may indulge my title, *The Trouble with Confucianism,* and accept its intended ambiguity with respect to the word "trouble." This is meant to include the different kinds of trouble Confucianism either fell into, made for itself, or created for others. In my view, as a way of life and a continuing discourse, Confucianism was a problematical enterprise from its inception, and, as it responded to the challenges of each age, addressing some perhaps better than others, it had both successes and failures. Looked at in this way, the "good and bad points of Confucianism" tend to go together. Rather than thinking of them as fixed points in a static system, we might better view them as mirroring each other in a convoluted historical process, as constants and continuities in the midst of discontinuities and difficulties.

Further, if we think of "trouble" as what was wrong or went wrong with Confucianism, our first consideration must be to ask, "By what measure?" My answer is that any failure should, in the first instance, be judged by the standards and goals Confucians put before themselves. Simply to establish such criteria will be more of a task than most of us have realized, but it takes priority over any other historical judgment we might hope to render.

Finally, I should mention that among the topics to which Confucianism gave priority or special attention, one would have to include rulership and leadership, scholarship and the school, the family and human relations, rites and religion. Within the limits of the present essays I shall focus on the first, leadership, with lesser reference to scholarship and religion, but hardly any to the family. This, as it happened, was the order in which Confucius first addressed these topics. The family and what I call "human rites" are important, and cannot be left wholly out of account here, but they are also important enough to deserve separate and fuller attention than can be given in these pages.

"The trouble with Confucianism" has been a lifetime problem with me. During my student days in the late thirties and forties, two divergent views of Confucianism prevailed: one fashionable view, in the West as in China, held it responsible for most of China's modern ills; the other opinion, held in less political circles, saw Confucius as the quintessential Chinese sage. This latter view was not to be found only in fortune cookies; writers with some claim on an educated reader's attention—Lin Yutang, Herrlee Creel, and, in the eyes of those who admired his poetry, Ezra Pound—were among those who appreciated Confucius' teachings as virtually ageless. Nor was the critical view held only by radicals and revolutionaries bent on trashing the old order; liberals and social scientists tended, if not to belittle Confucianism, at least to treat it as a matter best left to fusty Orientalists.

These two views, though disparate, easily coexisted. Confucius himself was safely ensconced far back in the sixth century B.C., to be admired at a distance, while his followers were unceremoniously dumped, ages away, in a nineteenth-century world mired in dynastic corruption. Across this historical gulf, the twain simply did not meet. Few holding either view gave much thought to what happened in between or asked how a teaching so timeless could have come to such an untimely and unworthy end. Moderns easily believed that the Middle Ages were Dark Ages anyhow, blighted by a nameless plague. Those whose faith was all in the future could admire the past, but only a past remote enough not to pose troubling questions for that future.

More recently, the day I received an invitation to deliver the first of the Tanner Lectures at the University of California, Berkeley, on a topic of "broad, general interest," it also happened that Jacques Barzun asked me large questions about the Confucian past which I could not hope to answer in a luncheon conversation; but, being still in the habit of responding to a teacher's questions, I decided to do so in the Tanner Lectures, which might someday be available to him in print. The germ of this book, then, consisted of the lectures delivered in Berkeley in May 1988. They have since been expanded considerably in other lectures given at the Institute of East Asian Philosophies at the University of Singapore, in a paper presented to a conference on Confucianism and Christianity in Hong Kong, June 1988, and in discussions with the Society of Senior Scholars at Columbia's Heyman Center for the Humanities. Portions of Chapter 4 are drawn from lectures originally given at the Collège de France in May 1986; they are reprinted here from my *Message of the Mind* (1989) by permission of Columbia University Press. For helpful comments and suggestions I wish to thank particularly Professors David Johnson of the University of California, Berkeley; Wu Teh-yao and Lin Yu-sheng in Singapore; Jacques Gernet of the Collège de France; Thomas Metzger of the University of California, San Diego; and my colleagues at Columbia, Irene Bloom, Wing-tsit Chan, Louis Henkin, Joseph Mazzeo, and David Weiss-Halivni.

Unless otherwise indicated the translations herein are my own, but in the case of Confucius' *Analects,* so frequently quoted in the early chapters, "my own" here does not exclude the possibility of some influence from the translations of James Legge, Arthur Waley, and D. C. Lau, whom I have regularly consulted over the years.

The Trouble with
Confucianism

1

Sage-Kings
and Prophets

THE TROUBLE with Confucianism was there from the start, to become both a perennial challenge and a dilemma that would torment it through history—there in the founding myths of the tradition as the ideal of humane governance, and thereafter even in Confucianism's moments of apparent worldly success, as the ungovernable reality of imperial rule. When we encounter it first in the classic *Book of Documents'* "Canon of Yao," we find this idealization of the sage-king:

> Examining into antiquity, we find that the Emperor Yao was named Fang-hsun. He was reverent, intelligent, accomplished, ~ *educat.* sincere and mild. He was genuinely respectful and capable of all modesty. His light spread over the four extremities of the world, extending to Heaven above and Earth below. He was able to make bright his great virtue and bring affection to the nine branches of the family. When the nine branches of the family had become harmonious, he distinguished and honored the great clans. When the hundred clans had become illustrious, he harmonized the myriad states. Thus the numerous peoples were amply nourished, prospered, and became harmonious.[1]

No depth of insight is required to see embodied here in Yao all the civilized virtues of a good Confucian ruler; his reverent and respectful manner, his intelligence, his disciplined attainments, his self-restraint and modesty, his concern for others—all having a marvelous efficacy in the moral transformation of his people, all manifest in the beneficent power of his paternal care, radiating from the luminous center of his personal virtue, outward through successive degrees of kinship to distant states and the very ends of the world, harmonizing all mankind in one loving family and bringing them into a cosmic unity with Heaven and Earth.

Note, however, what is simply given, what is so naturally assumed in the presentation of this heroic ideal: its setting is altogether a human world, a familial order, with its patriarchal leader already in place and, what is more, already in place at the center. There is no creation myth here, no Genesis. Even as a founding myth, the Canon of Yao projects neither conquest nor struggle; neither antagonist, nor rival to overcome, nor any countervailing power to be met. The sage-king stands alone, unchallenged and unchecked except by self-imposed restraints. And in the sequel to this account of Yao's commanding virtue, the question is simply one of finding a worthy successor. There is nothing contested, no problem except how to find another paragon of humble virtue to whom rulership may be entrusted.

Whether or not this founding myth of the Confucians, as an ideal of rulership by individual merit rather than by right of inheritance, served as an implicit, desacralizing critique of the established order, as seems likely, it remained quite susceptible of appropriation by the patriarchal, dynastic state itself. The fact that the Canon of Yao was much later found to be an imposition upon the original *Documents* detracts neither from its mythic function in the Confucian tradition concerning the sage-kings, nor, given the assumption of unitary rule, from its adaptation to the ideological purposes of imperial sages. For the myth and the reality of unitary rule were more than just Confucian. Before Confucius put his own distinctive impress on them, they were waiting for him in the record of China's primordial age. Much of the classical canon itself antedates Confucius, and others of the pre-Confucian texts celebrate the ideal of the sage-king, as does this passage from the *Book of Odes* eulogizing King Wen, a founder-father of the Chou dynasty, as bearer of Heaven's mandate:

> King Wen is on high;
> Oh, he shines in Heaven
> . . . August was King Wen
> Continuously bright and reverent.
> Great indeed was his mandate from Heaven.[2]

In Confucius' passing down of the Odes and other classics to later generations, there is reason to credit what he says of himself in the *Analects*—that he was a faithful transmitter of tradition. In this case, the idea of the sage-king was a Chinese reality before it became a Confucian myth. Archeological evidence confirms the suspicion that centralized rule and the dominance of a single ruler, combining religious and political authority, were already facts of historical life before Confucius came on the scene. That this centralized rule was already rationalized and bureaucratized to a high degree, as David Keightley's recent studies confirm,[3] warrants the view that late Shang dynasty China already prefigured the characteristic imperial order of the Ch'in and Han in this important respect: it entailed a symmetrical structure of power, with varying degrees of control or autonomy at the outer reaches, but converging on a center of increasing density, though not always of heightened power, in terms of bureaucratic administration, economic control, and cultural influence. True enough, this centralizing trend would reach a new threshold at the end of the Chou and would become further rationalized in the Ch'in and Han, yet such increasing concentration of power implies no radical discontinuity from the past. Even the "feudal order" or enfeoffment system looked, at least in theory, to such a commissioning, if not commanding, center. As Hsü Cho-yün has characterized this "feudal order," kingship stood at the center of a vast kinship organization, coupled with a strong state structure.[4]

Thus we are not surprised to find that such a pyramid of authority is accepted implicitly in the *Analects* (16:2): "When the Way prevails in the world, rites, music, and punishments issue from the Son of Heaven. When the Way does not prevail, these issue from the feudal lords. When they issue from the feudal lords, one cannot but expect power to pass from the Son of Heaven within ten generations. When they issue from the Great Officers, one cannot but expect power to pass from the feudal lords in five generations."

The Noble Man as Counterpoint to the Sage-King

In the Ode to King Wen quoted earlier there is another stanza addressed to the scions of the Chou house, which refers to the Shang dynasty's loss of Heaven's Mandate to the Chou:

> The charge is not easy to keep
> May it not end in your persons
> Display and make bright your good fame
> And consider what Yin [the Shang] had received from
>   Heaven [and then lost].
> The moral burden of high Heaven
> Is unwritten, unspoken.
> Take King Wen as your model
> And the people will trust in you.[5]

Here the power of the ruling house is subject to the intangible moral restraint which Heaven imposes as the unstated condition of the Chou's exercise of sovereignty. While King Wen stands as the model of such restraint, the moral burden falls on his house, his descendants, as a public and collective responsibility.

When, in the *Analects,* we encounter the same charge, it assumes a new form. The idea of power held in public trust is still there, but when Confucius talks about Heaven's Mandate he does not address a ruling house, urging fidelity to the example of its founder as a condition of its longevity and tenure. Rather, the Mandate has been reconceived as an individual mission and personal commitment to the service of humankind in the broadest sense. Confucius speaks of this to his students and companions as members of an educated elite with a high calling to leadership and public service, even when they hold no power. For them Heaven's imperative (*t'ien-ming*) is no dynastic commission but a claim on their individual political and moral conscience.

By the same token or tally the sage-king as model for a dynasty has little direct relevance for Confucius and his followers, who, with the decline of the old aristocracy, are hardly in a position to emulate it. More pertinent is the example of the noble man (*chün-tzu*),[6] who may now hold no office at all. This is not because he lacks a vocation to public service but because, unlike the scions of the Chou in former times, the noble man may be politically displaced or unrecognized. Heaven may not have destined him for office or disposed of his personal circumstances so as to give him direct access to power or political influence.

Here we see a change taking place in the meaning of the term *chün-tzu*. Formerly indicating membership in a declining hereditary aristocracy, it comes to stand for a new class committed to public service through the cultivation of individual moral and intellectual virtues. From someone highborn, the *chün-tzu* is transformed into someone high-minded. No longer the privileged offspring of an upper class, he is set apart and above the lower order of small-minded men (*hsiao-jen*) by his largeness of heart and moral stature. *in a way like the noble Emperors -(u.class but rule by virtue only)*

In this transition from the old order to the new, an underlying continuity is to be found in the idea of good breeding as refined cultivation among the leadership elite. Arthur Waley saw this development as paralleling the evolution of the English gentleman from a social aristocrat to an individual of exemplary conduct—a parallel even more apt in Waley's day, when the concept of the English gentleman still carried with it a strong sense of honor and a demanding code of conduct. Today, when the concept of the gentleman is much weaker, the two-fold sense of continuity and change, of tradition in the process of transition, may in certain contexts be better conveyed by making a distinction between nobleman and Noble Man—this for want of a single term in English that expresses both the new emphasis on the *chün-tzu*'s distinctive individual worth and the surviving sense of strong group or class identity that comes from a shared commitment to public service and the upholding of a civilized tradition.[7]

noblesse oblige

civilized upper class

In later tradition Confucius is often spoken of as a sage, even as personifying the ultimate in sagehood. Indeed, mention of "the Sage" in later literature usually points back to Confucius. But if Confucius is seen as embodying the quintessence of sagely wisdom, in the *Analects* itself Confucius has little to say about the sage or sageliness. In fact, the few references we have to it put sagehood on a level beyond ordinary human reach—important as an ultimate ideal but attainable only if one first sets about achieving the more proximate goal of becoming a noble man.

"A sage it has not been mine to see," Confucius says; "could I just see a noble man that would be enough" (7:26). Again, when Confucius' disciple Tzu Kung asks, "Suppose there were someone who benefited all the people and aided the multitudes, could he be called 'humane'?" Confucius responds, "What has that to do with humaneness? One would have to be a sage to accomplish that. Even

*remark all[?]
reyton's[?] famli[?]
rites[?] Mankind[?]*

Yao and Shun had concerns like these" (6:30). Confucius goes on then to talk about how one should start with oneself and those nearest to one, following the principle of mutuality or reciprocity, as the way to achieve humaneness, rather than by any attempt directly to emulate the sages.

True, the noble man had to keep the model of the sages constantly before him. Of the three things a noble man should hold in awe, the words of the sages are one, along with the imperatives of Heaven and the example of great men (16:8). But Confucius makes no pretense to sageliness or perfect virtue himself. He says, "Sagely and humane—how dare I think of myself as such? Of me it could only be said that I strive to emulate such qualities and to teach others unswervingly" (7:33). And when a high officer asked Tzu Kung if his master was not a sage, Tzu Kung acknowledged that indeed Confucius was a man of many parts. Yet Confucius, on hearing of this, demurred and questioned its underlying assumption. "Need the noble man be a person of many parts?" he asked, implying that, while the fullness of human perfection was a hallmark of the sage, those who, like himself, would aspire to be noble men, need not, and would best not, think of themselves as aiming at the omnicompetence of the sage (a defining characteristic of sagehood, as seen also in 19:12).

By contrast to the half-dozen references to sagehood which tend to elevate it out of reach, the *Analects* offer no less than 106 passages dealing with the subject of the noble man. From these passages one can draw a fair picture of the noble man as Confucius conceived of him, something I attempt to do in Chapter 2. Here I confine myself to a few points.

The first is that even if Confucius be considered a sage and his teachings thought universal, they are still defined in part by his audience, inasmuch as Confucius addresses himself in the first instance to a specific social class—the educated leadership class of his own time—and offers that class the concept of the noble man as its life ideal. As the central model of the *Analects,* the *chün-tzu* tends also to establish a specific focus for our understanding of Confucius' other teachings. Thus, though much in those teachings can be considered of universal value, as judged by their acceptance in cultures very different from the Chinese—Korean, Japanese, and Vietnamese especially—how we understand them and their possible relevance to other historical and cultural situations depends upon how well we understand Confucius' own situation and that of his genteel audience.

As one example, at international scholarly conferences these days, it has become the fashion to quote the opening lines of the *Analects,* which celebrate learning and friendship; rarely, however, does anyone quote the immediately following line about what it means to be truly a noble man, crucial though that concluding line is to comprehending the full meaning of what precedes it. Almost anyone can share Confucius' sentiments about learning and friendship, but without some understanding of the historical circumstances of the *chün-tzu,* and how Confucius redefined the concept of true leadership, it may be more difficult to appreciate the full depth of the question Confucius is posing for us.

What we have here is indeed the opening bid in Confucius' discussion of the noble man fulfilling his personal moral mission even in political adversity, simply by preserving his own self-respect and remaining true to his interior sense of what it is right and proper for him to do. In this opening passage he asks the question whether truly being a noble man does not mean remaining unsoured even if one is unknown or unrecognized (*Analects* 1). The normal expectation for the *chün-tzu* would be that he receive some recognition (that is, position) from the ruler, yet Confucius pointedly subordinates the outward status (the political or social standing of the nobleman) to the inner nobility and peace of mind of the noble man. The one-time aristocrat, now "unknown" and politically a nobody, could make something of himself by becoming a truly noble man.

Confucius stresses the point again by speaking of the noble man as one who stands by his professed principles, his dedication to the True Way, no matter what ignominious fate he may suffer. "He is never so harried, never so endangered, but that he cleaves to this" (*Analects* 4:5). This requires more than the courteous behavior of the gentleman. Uncompromising adherence to principle cannot be served simply by a nice diffidence or polite disengagement from human affairs. A life of continuing struggle may be called for. When it is suggested that Confucius abandon his efforts to reform rulers, he counters by asserting the need to persist even against the indifference of those in power. "If the Way prevailed in the world [that is, simply of itself, without the need for conscientious effort on man's part], I would not be trying to change things" (*Analects* 18:6).

Confucius had already been derided for "fleeing from this man and that" (meaning: avoiding service to one ruler or another), when, as he was advised, he would do better "to flee from this whole generation of men" (that is, give up on political reform altogether). His response was neither to give up nor to give in, neither to retire from the scene in order fastidiously to preserve his inner integrity, nor, on the other hand, to accept whatever office might be available simply for the sake of keeping himself politically occupied and comfortably provided for. Rather, peripatetically on the political circuit of ancient China, Confucius traveled the twisting road that lay between easy accommodation and total withdrawal.

Given this example of Confucius and his portrayal of the noble man, one understands how later Confucians would have had to stray rather far from the Master's precepts if they were to fit Max Weber's characterization of the Confucian as a gentleman politely accommodating himself to the status quo or rationally adjusting to the world in which he found himself.[8] True, the modest, respectful manner and careful prudential conduct expected of the Confucian *chün-tzu* lend some plausibility to Weber's view. But if the Confucian is worldly and urbane in this respect, he, like Confucius, must heed the imperatives of Heaven as the supreme moral order in the universe, and answer to it in his conscience. "He who offends against Heaven has none to whom he can pray" (*Analects* 3:3). In Confucius' account of his own life-experience, the ultimate meaning and value of his mission in life is bound up with "recognizing the imperatives of Heaven" and "learning to follow them" (*Analects* 2:4). "There are," he says, "three things of which the noble man stands in awe: the imperatives of Heaven, great men, and the words of the sages" (15:8). And finally, in the last lines of the *Analects,* Confucius says, "Unless one recognizes the imperatives of Heaven, one cannot be a noble man" (20:3).

It is this compelling voice of conscience and ideal standard represented by the imperatives of Heaven which serves as the ultimate criterion and court of judgment in assessing human affairs. According to the Confucian conception of humanity or humaneness (*jen*), man can indeed be the measure of man, but it is only because this high moral sense and cosmic dimension of the human mind-and-heart give it the capacity for self-transcendence. Likewise, if the Confucian, even while accepting the world, still hopes to gain the leverage on it necessary for its transformation, Heaven's imperative in the minds of men serves as the fulcrum. So it is, too, with the stance of the noble man, standing on the same moral ground at court, hoping to transform the ruler.

Recognizing this potential transformative power in Confucian thought, the neo-Weberian sociologist Shmuel Eisenstadt has amended Weber's characterization of Confucianism, calling it now, quite seriously though paradoxically, a "this-worldly transcendentalism."[9] Thus Eisenstadt acknowledges the tension between the given world and Heaven's imperative, a tension expressed by Confucius when, ridiculed for his unrealism and still unwilling either to accommodate or abandon the rulers of his day, he insisted on the need both for himself and for them to make the Way prevail in the world.

In earlier works of mine I have drawn attention to what I call the "prophetic voice" in the later Confucian tradition—in the Neo-Confucianism of the Sung and after—which questioned received tradition in the form of Han and T'ang Confucian scholarship, and judged severely the politics of the late imperial dynasties in China. Without intending any exact or entire equation of the Confucian noble voice with prophetic utterance in the more theistic traditions, wherein the prophet has often renounced the world and "gone out into the desert," I wished to show that even a world-affirming Confucian could render severe judgments on the established order, asserting absolute claims on behalf of inner conscience. As I said of this distinction:

"Prophetic" I use here to indicate an extraordinary access to and revelation of truth not vouchsafed to everyone, which by some process of inner inspiration or solitary perception affords an insight beyond what is received in scripture, and by appeal to some higher order of truth gives new meaning, significance, and urgency to certain cultural values or scriptural texts. Confucian tradition does not customarily speak of such a revelation as "supernatural," but it has an unpredictable, wondrous quality manifesting the divine creativity of Heaven. By contrast I use "scholastic" to represent an appeal to received authority by continuous transmission, with stress on external or public acceptance of it as the basis of its validity.[10]

Max Weber defined "prophet" primarily in contrast to "priest": "We shall understand 'prophet' to mean a purely individual bearer of charisma, who by virtue of his mission proclaims a religious doctrine or divine commandment . . . The personal call is the decisive element distinguishing prophet from priest. The latter lays claim to authority by virtue of service in a sacred tradition, while the prophet's claim is based on personal revelation and charisma."[11]

In the Confucian case the claim to authority is usually based on a received and revered scholarly tradition that, from time to time, is challenged by some individual prophetic revelation, but then comes to incorporate elements of the new message in itself. In this sense Julia Ching in her comparative study *Confucianism and Christianity* is entitled to speak of some Confucians as prophets:

> Confucianism has never known an organized, ecclesiastical priesthood. The emperor was the mediator between Heaven and the people, by virtue of his position as political ruler. He was assisted by his ministers—an educated bureaucracy of men versed in rituals and ethics. Together, they represented a kind of lay priesthood, although their dignity and mission flowed more from their education and merit than from any personal charisma. They constituted a special class in society, representing a commitment to service of state and society, in the name of the common good. They were sometimes called "gentlemen" (*chün-tzu*). Time and again, from among these ranks, a "prophet" would emerge who raised his voice of protest against misrule, directing his complaints to the "kings" as did his Hebrew counterparts. Such a man would be a true follower of Confucius and Mencius. Such a man would speak in the name of the Classics, the sages, and of Heaven.[12]

With respect to Confucius himself, D. C. Lau says: "Anyone who has read the sayings of Confucius carefully and without prejudice will surely find it difficult to recognize the die-hard conservative and arch-villain that he has sometimes been made out to be. Confucius is perhaps yet another instance of the proverbial prophet." [13]

The later Neo-Confucian development has its own distinctive features, shown especially in its teaching concerning the mind, which dismisses the received authority of Han and T'ang classical scholarship as mindless antiquarianism, and strikes out in new directions. Equally—and more importantly—it rejects the Ch'an Buddhist view of the mind. In either case, the prophetic voice in Neo-Confucianism disavows lineal descent or direct inheritance, but stresses the mind's direct access to the Way, as in the term "Learning of the Way" (*tao-hsüeh*), which asserts the primary and absolute claims of this direct knowledge of the Way, as principles implanted in the human mind, in contrast to learning received through cultural inheritance (*wen*).

In the classical period, we are dealing with a prophetic voice in a more basic sense—that is, the direct perception and inspired utterance of truths concerning the course of human events and the dire consequences of flouting the moral order decreed by Heaven. Here Heaven itself does not speak like the God of the Old Testament, nor does it personally direct the actions of a "prophet." In that respect it would be misleading to call the Confucian noble man a prophet. But if "Heaven does not speak" (*Analects* 17:17) in the way Yahweh spoke to the prophets of the Old Testament, and consequently man is left to speak for Heaven, still Heaven's Decree or Ordinance (*t'ien-ming*) connotes in the character for *ming* an oral command to be executed by human agency, and asserts an ordaining authority that warrants the individual's claim to speak out on behalf of Heaven. Thus, the noble man does have his own personal mission to uphold a moral order identified with the celestial order—Heaven's creative, directive, governing, and punishing power in the form of *t'ien-ming*. It is the noble man, then, who speaks for Heaven, obeying the dictates of Heaven's imperative as expressed in the individual human mind, and laying on the ruler Heaven's censure of actions contrary to the Way.

These, then, are the elements in the prophetic role of the Confucian noble man which give him some resemblance to prophets of the Semitic world: direct, individual perception of the Way as a transcendent value; the inspired utterance of the noble man as witness to a Heaven that does not itself speak; the noble man's sense of mission—indeed, commission by Heaven; and the warning to rulers lest they bring destruction on themselves by disobeying Heaven's Mandate.

In this respect the Confucian may perform in the generic role of the prophet as a proclaimer of the truth. There is in what he proclaims something closely akin to the "justice and righteousness" that is so compelling a concern of the early Old Testament prophets. True, Confucian humaneness (*jen*) is not the exact equivalent of the love that God showers on mankind and that the latter is expected to reciprocate in acts of charity and mercy; nor is Confucian rightness (*i*) the same as Old Testament "righteousness," being more circumscribed by the particular circumstances surrounding an action than is the more abstract and transcendental Judeo-Christian concept of "righteousness." Yet when Confucius and Mencius condemn acts of inhumanity and unrightness on the part of oppressive rulers, they speak with a prophetic voice sounding much like Hosea, Joel, Amos, and Nahum among the prophets of the Old Testament.

Notwithstanding this important resemblance, however, there are good reasons to distinguish this prophetic Confucian voice from the role of the prophet and prophetic message in Ancient Israel. Some of the more obvious differences in the message are the following: There is no personal God directly intervening in history, a God with whom the prophet might be said to have some personal relation, engage in mutual dialogue, and even "wrestle." Lacking here is any sense of the people's responsibility to Heaven as "a people," comparable to the responsibility of God's people specially called to fulfill the Covenant in the Old Testament. No prospect of fulfillment or reward beckons in the future, no threat of final judgment and damnation as in Christianity and Islam links past and present to future in the Confucian view of history. The ruler and his dynasty alone are made to bear responsibility for the sufferings of the people; there is no scolding of the people themselves for breaches of faith or derelictions of duty, nor are the people's sufferings seen as retribution visited upon them for their own sins. Visions and ecstatic experiences that authenticate a prophet's calling are rare in Confucianism, which more typically appeals to ordinary human experience. In all these ways then—and no doubt others besides—the prophetic message or voice as found among the Confucians may be distinguished from that of the prophets known to Judaism, Christianity, and Islam.

Some of these differences are highly significant for the development of Chinese history and society. History, for all its importance to the Chinese, has a quite different meaning for them without any concept of the covenant, of God's personal intervention in time, of a Messianic fulfillment. No linear view of history from covenant to apocalypse, from B.C. to A.D. and on to the Second Coming, orients all time toward a millenarian or apocalyptic finale. Only in the twentieth century does the advent of the prophetic view, as brought to China with Christianity and Marxism, usher in a new revolutionary age, predicated on a cumulative or progressive view, looking to the future. Until then in East Asia time is measured in seasonal or sexagenary cycles, or, for purposes of the secular chronicler, by dynasties and the reign titles of rulers. In other words, time is subject to the dominion of temporal rulers. For the Buddhists time has little significance because it is transitory and ephemeral; for the most part they leave the writing of history to others and do not challenge the ruler's hold over secular time. In the West time belongs to the prophets, being measured from the Creation according to Moses, the birth of Christ, or the hegira of Muhammad. In Confucian East Asia time belongs to the emperors and kings. (The famous *Tale of Genji* begins with the Japanese equivalent of "once upon a time": "In whatever reign it was, . . ." Literally the text speaks of "august time," but "august" is understood to mean imperial.)

Another circumstance of Confucius' audience highly significant for our understanding of his message is the fact that he speaks in a scholarly and collegial setting. The aphorisms and anecdotes of the *Analects* reveal a continuing intimate dialogue or discussion among friends and disciples. Confucius is not declaiming before a crowd or preaching to an assembled congregation. He is not exhorting the masses. He is engaged in intimate converse, appealing to shared personal experience of life among a few persons of largely similar status and background.

For comparison we may consider what is said about this matter in John F. A. Sawyer's recent book, which presents itself as a scholarly overview of recent studies concerning "prophecy and the prophets of the Old Testament."[14] On the one hand, Sawyer denies that there was a great gap in social background and education between the prophets and the political and religious establishment. He says that the evidence points in the direction of educated prophets from a background not dissimilar to that of other leaders, officials and members of the intelligentsia. However emphatically they may protest their independence from the 'establishment,' their style, their knowledge, and their prominent role in society prove that they belonged to the religious, political, and educational heart of ancient Israelite society."[15]

Having thus disputed the conventional view of the prophets as standing free of the religious establishment, Sawyer curiously dismisses any notion that either the prophets' stance vis-à-vis established institutions, or their involvement with these, had any bearing on the prophetic message one way or the other. What specially marked the prophets was not their behavior, their role in society, or their education, but the content of their teaching and their experience of God, "their opposition to the official cult came from their moral and religious convictions, not from their different social background or status."[16]

If this leaves one to wonder, given the seeming free-floating character of the prophetic message, by what agency the message could have been carried, Sawyer has little to offer but doubt that the preservation and propagation of that message owed anything to disciples, guilds, or schools of followers, there being only one uncertain "reference to disciples in the whole corpus [of prophetic books in the Old Testament]."[17] Nothing could be more greatly in contrast than this to the situation of the Confucians, whose literature abounds in references to disciples, scholarly companies and lineages, and schools. This may well have some bearing on the further question, to be taken up later, of how the prophetic message in each case reached the people and was related to them.[18] Here we simply note that the bearers of the prophetic message in China are an educated elite marked by their commitment to scholarship and the school, to public service and participation in government. As such they may be differentiated to some degree from the prophets of Israel and the West, who appear to be more free-standing and less professionally committed to such secular functions.

Confucius is no Moses or Muhammad, conveying the direct words of a very personal God, but his critique of the rulers of his time appeals to the authority of high Heaven and invokes the ideal order of the sage-kings praised for their reverence and obedience to Heaven. Mencius, for his part, echoes strongly Confucius' views on Heaven, the ideal order of the sage-kings, and the role of the noble man in challenging the rulers of his day. Indeed he heightens considerably the tension between the Confucian ideals of humanity (*jen*) and rightness (*i*) and, by contrast, the brutal politics of his time. Notwithstanding his affirmation of the essential goodness of human nature, he was quick to expose the faults of contemporary rulers—their callousness, selfishness, pretentiousness, and even their minor failings. Nothing short of a scrupulous adherence to the Way was demanded. Even the sacrifice of one's life was not too much to ask of those who would live up to the full measure of their humanity (6A:10). For himself, Mencius insisted that even the gaining of power over the whole world would not justify killing one man or committing a single act of unrightness to accomplish it (2A:2). And of the noble man he said that among his three greatest pleasures in life, to rule the world would not be one of them (these are the three: that his parents still be alive and his brothers well, that he feel no shame over his own conduct, and that he have able students—7A:20).

By no means the last Confucian to speak in these idealistic terms, Mencius was probably the first to express realistically what would be required of ministers who sought to convey the Confucian message to rulers. No one has exposed more forthrightly than he the danger of cooptation that lay in the ruler-minister relation or the seductive ease with which officials could fall into the obsequiousness of servitors or slaves, awed by autocratic power. Like Confucius, he distinguished between true nobility, identified with moral and intellectual worth, and the superficialities of worldly rank. The former he called the "nobility of Heaven" (*t'ien-chüeh*), again identifying high moral standards with Heaven. Worldly rank he termed the "nobility of men," empty and ephemeral unless grounded in man's inborn moral sense and reflective of a hierarchy of true values.[19] No one inveighed so fearlessly as Mencius against the pretensions of power and prestige (though admittedly this could be seen as more the fearlessness of the teacher in a classroom than that of the minister at court or the soldier in battle). "Those who counsel the great should view them with contempt and not have regard for their pomp and display. Lofty halls with great beams—these, even if successful, I would not have. Quantities of food, hundreds of girls in attendance—these, even if successful, I would not have . . . What they [princes] have, is nothing I would have. What I would have is the restraints and regulations of the ancients. Why should I stand in awe of princes?"[20]

The relationship between prince and minister should be based on mutual respect, not subservience of the latter to the former. Quoting the *Odes,* Mencius said, "To take one's prince to task is to show one's respect for him" (4A:1). In turn, the prince should treat his counsellors with all the respect due a teacher, and the latter should hold himself aloof from a ruler who failed to show sufficient deference. In ancient times it was not counsellors who sought out rulers but the other way around. Wise and virtuous counsellors who sought out rulers in antiquity "delighted in the Way and were oblivious to the power of princes. Therefore if kings and dukes did not show respect or fulfill what was required by rites, they would not even get to visit the wise and virtuous, much less have the latter come to see them" (6B:8). And of the ruler's treatment of the *chün-tzu* at court, Mencius said: "To feed him and not love him is to treat him as a pig. To love him and not respect him is to treat him as a pet. Respect must come before gifts. Respect not substantiated in action can only be taken by the noble man as an empty gesture."[21] In this way Mencius attempted to invest the Confucian noble man as minister and official with the privileged position necessary for him to serve as independent counsel, and thus provide a counterpoint to the dictates of the ruler.

With or without such a position, however, Mencius felt compelled to speak out against injustice and misrule. Charged with being fractious and disputatious, he insisted that he had no alternative but to speak out so long as the Way of the Sage-Kings did not prevail in the world (3B:9). As with the prophets, it was his duty to serve as a warner to others. Quoting the sage-minister I Yin, he said, "Heaven in giving birth to the people has given to those who first understand the duty of arousing those slow to understand, and to those who first awaken the duty of awakening those slow to awaken. I am among the first of Heaven's people to awaken, I shall awaken this people by means of the Way." [22]

Mencius' vision was of a regime no less unitary than that attributed to the sage-kings, whose ideal order he too evoked, but Mencius could conceive of a center that did not arrogate all power to itself, balanced by an autonomous feudal nobility and ministered to by truly noble men, exercising this independent prophetic function as a counterweight to the concentration of power and wealth in the ruler.

The question that comes to mind, when one considers the prophetic function as a counterweight to the ruler, is what the nature of the countervailing force might be. Weber, as we have seen, believed that the two essential ingredients of the prophetic claim lay in personal revelation and charisma.[23] The Confucians, though they claimed no direct revelation from a personal God, did not want for personal inspiration. As for charisma, Confucius and Mencius would not seem to have lacked a certain personal magnetism, but the evidence of it is chiefly how they moved or impressed their disciples. Julia Ching, above, makes no great claim for the Confucians on this score, saying their effect "flowed more from their education and merit than from personal charisma." What this points to is the school and the court as the social locale of the Confucian prophetic function. But what is left to be explained is how either the prophetic message or charisma related to the people.

God's People/Heaven's People

Just how the charisma of the Old Testament prophets worked, and upon whom it had its effect, are questions perhaps inherently difficult to answer, given the intangible and elusive nature of charisma. On the evidence of the prophetic books, however, one thing is certain: the people are centrally and directly involved, whether they be spoken of as God's people, the people of Israel, or the tribes and cities of Israel. Everywhere the theme of the prophets is God's love for his people, his solicitude for them, his jealous demands, his anger, his forgiveness of them. And throughout these repeated scoldings and exhortations of the people, this intense personal concern of God for them is given voice in a passionate eloquence that is the special mark of religious literature in the Semitic traditions. This is most true of the prophets who speak of the Covenant between God and his people. When we hear the voice of the prophet appealing to God's people or berating the people of Israel, it is almost impossible to conceive of this polemic as uttered except to some actual throng, assemblage, or congregation.

The same sense of terrible urgency, of the need to move people to action, the intensity of personal involvement on the part of the prophet with God and his people, recurs in the writings of Abraham Heschel:

> The prophet's theme is, first of all, the very life of a whole people, and his identification with it lasts more than a moment. He is one not only with what he says; he is involved with his people in what his words foreshadow . . . Above all the prophets remind us of the moral state of the people. Few are guilty, but all are responsible . . . Great orators in Rome had frequently manifested courage in publicly condemning the abuse of power by individuals. But the prophets challenge the whole country: kings, priests, false prophets, and the entire nation.[24]

From this it is plain that for the prophets, "the people" means every individual and all the people. No one is exempted from the responsibility.

When we turn to the Confucian case, there is much evidence of a prime concern for the people (*min*) and every reason to believe that both the people's welfare and the people's sufferings weigh heavily on the Confucian conscience. Mencius comes immediately to mind because of his often cited doctrine of the "people's right of revolution," based on his willingness to condone the overthrow of tyrants by the people they have abused. Yet the people loom no less large in the thinking of Confucius and in that of the other great Confucian of the late Chou period, Hsün Tzu, who likened the ruler to a boat and the people to the water that may either sustain or overturn the ruler.

There is then no need to belabor the importance of the people in Confucian thought. What does require attention is the relation of the people to the ruler and to the noble man as prophet. And when the question is raised, against the background of the prophetic books of the Old Testament, surprising things stand out in comparative light.

A typical Confucian view of the people in relation to Heaven— that is, "Heaven's people" as the relevant comparison to "God's people" in the Old Testament—is found in the *Tso Chuan* commentary on the *Spring and Autumn Annals:* "Heaven gave birth to the people and set up rulers to superintend and shepherd them and see to it that they do not lose their true nature as human beings. And because there are rulers, it provided helpers for them who would teach and protect them and see that they do not overstep the bounds." The passage goes on to assert that in ancient times a similar process of assistance and criticism was encouraged on each level of society, comparable to the correction of the ruler by his ministers and teachers: "Heaven's love for the people is very great. Would it then allow one man to preside over them in an arrogant and wilful manner, indulging his excesses and casting aside the nature Heaven and Earth allotted them? Surely it would not!"

Here, without quite the fire and passion of the Old Testament prophets, Heaven's parentage of the people and its paternal solicitude are invoked in judgment upon the ruler. Burton Watson, whose translation I am quoting, comments that this "is a highly enlightened sermon on the responsibility of rulership and the need for all groups in society to seek correction from their kin and associates."[25] It is also clear from the opening lines that Heaven entrusts to the ruler and his ministers the responsibility for engendering and encouraging this process of mutual correction and consolation.

In the *Analects* itself there are fifty-two references to the *min,* the most common term for "people," understood as the common people, the multitudes. *Jen* may also be understood as the people at large, referring to humanity in the most universal sense, embracing all peoples. Not surprisingly in a work which is primarily concerned with the noble man and his leadership responsibilities, the great majority of references to *min* involve their relationship to the ruler, but the point of these is most often to underscore the responsibility of the ruler and the noble man for leading and caring for the people, while the *min* are generally spoken of as the undifferentiated mass of common people dependent on the actions of those in power. Though by no means purely passive, the activity of the common people is a reflex of the ruler's initiatives. They either follow him gladly, remain sullen or resistant, or perhaps rebel.

Almost without exception, Confucius' attitude is sympathetic to the common people and admonitory toward the ruler. He talks about the responsibility of the ruler for the people entrusted to him by Heaven—and elsewhere of the responsibility of the people for one another—but not of the people's answerability to Heaven or their obligation to remedy suffering and injustice. No doubt this reflects a basic difference between the educated leadership elite and the uneducated masses, but in any case it underscores the need for education to develop in leaders the personal qualities that will win them the people's confidence and support (usually expressed in terms of following, obeying, serving, or yielding to them).

These qualities or capacities of the *chün-tzu* may be summarized as follows:

1. His manifesting of virtue in forms that benefit the people. (*Analects* 15:34, 20:2)
2. His ability to command respect because of his own respectful or reverential manner. (6:30)
3. His cultivation of riteness—a disciplined observance of the social and religious forms that should govern the common life. Respect for rites and respect for the people are all of one piece. (1:9; 12:2; 13:4; 14:44)
4. His kindly, generous, and forbearing manner in dealing with the people. (18:2; 11:24)
5. His sense of confidence and trust in relations with the people. (12:7; 13:4; 15:25)
6. His reasonableness in making demands on the people, according to the seasons and circumstances. (19:10)
7. His zeal for learning and readiness to take responsibility for the education of the people. (6:20; 13:4; 13:29)

It is assumed that the people will follow leaders exhibiting such qualities. Chapter 8:9 says the people can be made to follow but cannot be expected to understand (the reasons for what they are asked to do) and thus, according to the commentary, are not to be held responsible. On the other hand, people should not be sent into battle without proper training or instruction (13:29, 30). Obviously there were some things the people could be expected to understand. Either way it left a responsibility for the *chün-tzu* to direct or instruct them. Thus there was a division of labor and specialization of function. Confucius has no hesitation in identifying himself as a man of learning who does not bother with farming, gardening, or military affairs (13:4, 15:1, 15:31). This is later confirmed by Mencius, who justified the scholar-official's freedom from the heavy bodily exertions of the peasant on the ground that the former could not discharge his leadership responsibilities unless he devoted himself to learning.

Differences in education had to be allowed for. Even though uneducated masses lacked the broad vision and depth of knowledge with which the *chün-tzu*'s education equipped him, the people's feelings still had to be taken into account. For, regardless of differences in education or social status, the people and their leaders shared the same basic moral sentiments and human needs.

Finally, it should be noted that nowhere in the *Analects,* so far as I am aware, does Confucius exhort, challenge, scold, or condemn the people. They are not to be blamed if things go wrong, but only to be accorded every sympathy, consideration, care, and protection. Only the ruler and his ministers are to be held accountable to Heaven, and the sufferings of the people are a reproach only to their leaders. As it comes from the *chün-tzu,* then, the prophetic voice is addressed only to the Son of Heaven and his officers. No such burden of conscience is laid on Heaven's people.

According to Ernest Nicholson, the crucial role of the prophets of Israel was to proclaim a radically new view, superseding a theology of creation which had sanctified the existing order and in particular had legitimated the ruler as the divinely appointed guardian of the establishment. The new prophetic view, by contrast, declares the goal of Israel, the very raison d'être of the nation, to be the fulfillment of God's righteousness. This view centered on the nature of God and of his will for Israel, and "what this demanded of Israel in response."[26] It became manifested in a covenant demanding Israel's exclusive allegiance to Yahweh. "Not merely the king-ship or any other institution but the social order as a whole was relativized in the face of a radicalized perception of Yahweh's righ-teousness."[27] It called for "a new understanding of Israel's exis-tence; from being a state among other states, Israel was conceived of as "the people of God, performing a role for God in history among the nations."[28]

As T. H. Robinson has said of the prophetic message of Amos:

> Israelite God as He was, (Yahweh) was still more the God of righ-teousness. His special relationship to his own people meant, not privilege to do wrong, but responsibility to do right . . . If (Israel) failed here—and this is the real essence of the teaching of Amos— she lost her only raison d'être, and so far from protecting her, Yah-weh would Himself ordain her ruin. Every nation, every sphere of life, was subject to these supreme laws, and the real function of Israel amongst the civilized peoples of the world was to work them out in the common life.[29]

The goal of the covenant thus became "the transformation of Israel from what it had historically been into what it had been sum-moned to be: the people of Yahweh."[30] A world thus "disen-chanted" (in the terms of Schiller and Weber—the insertion is mine) "is humanized in the sense that it becomes the arena for hu-man resolve and purposefulness, informed by God's will and in the service of God above."[31]

In the Confucian case, however, without such a covenant and without the people's becoming actively involved in fulfilling it, the responsibility for transforming the world falls entirely on the ruler and those who assist him. In other words the entire burden falls on the self-cultivation and self-transformation of the noble man. The same need for human resolve (chih) and purposefulness is there, but it is to have compassion on Heaven's people by achieving humane government (jen cheng) and doing what is right (i) by them. This was a burden no less heavy than that which fell on Israel, but with-out God's mercy and forgiveness available to rulers who failed.

The trouble with Confucianism at this level—and it was the chosen arena as well as the given level of Confucian thought and activity—was not that it gave too little scope or importance to the noble man as an individual but that it gave perhaps too much. It put upon him all the burden of responsibility that the prophets of Israel had laid on the whole people. If the noble man and the ruler were a trouble to each other, it was in large part because Confucius and Mencius held them accountable together for the troubles of the people.

As it is said of the noble man in the *Analects,* he "must be strong and resolute, for his burden of responsibility is heavy and the road is long. Taking upon himself the burden of humaneness, is that not heavy? Ceasing only at death, is that not long?" (8:7).

2

The Noble
Man in the
Analects

FROM WHAT HAS already been said about the prophetic role of the noble man, it should be clear that the trouble Confucians found themselves in arose precisely from the difficulty scholar-officials would experience in performing such a prophetic role. Yet another difficulty in reconciling such roles, for readers of the *Analects* at least, would lie in thinking of Confucius himself as a prophet. It is not so much that he made no claim to such authority, since his claiming almost nothing for himself has not kept later generations from investing him with titles to the most supreme authority, such as Ultimate Sage, Supreme Teacher, Uncrowned King, and so forth, to which could easily be added: Undeclared Prophet. More disconcerting perhaps for anyone who might think of the Sage as a prophet is his quiet, reserved manner and his cautious, tentative approach to truth. What prophet of the Old Testament, or indeed of any newer revelation, speaks with such nice diffidence? Or simply asks us if we do not agree with him? What revelation is it that is content merely to suggest what we should already know?

Let us return to the opening lines of the *Analects*. Each of Confucius' initial affirmations is in the form of a question. "To study and in due season to practice what one has learned—is this not a pleasure? To have friends come from afar—is this not a delight?" What could be more revealing of the gentleman-scholar who is at home with his culture, open and at ease with his friends? What could be more in keeping with Weber's characterization of the Confucian as a gentleman well-adjusted to his world?

But then, take the last sentence: "To be unsoured even if one is unrecognized—is this not to be a noble man (or true gentleman, *chün-tzu*)?" On the face of it the question issues from a reflective mind, not an agitated spirit, and is reassuring in its implied answer, its accepting tone. Confucius, we understand, is not despairing of his lot in life. On second thought, however, we note the possibility of the noble man's being unrecognized, which breaks into the harmony already asserted between himself, his culture, and other men. From a sharing in the learning of the past and in the experience of others, Confucius suddenly confronts us with a situation in which the *chün-tzu* faces rejection and must somehow stand on his own, compelled to draw on his inner resources rather than depend on others. Here then we encounter something like the proverbial solitariness of the prophet. As Confucius said of himself, not being understood by others, "Perhaps only Heaven understands me" (14:35).

We know from the *Analects'* frequent references to being unrecognized, to one's talents being unnoticed and unappreciated, that it was indeed a source of considerable anxiety for the gentlemen Confucius addressed (1:1, 1:16, 4:14, 11:24, 13:2, 14:17, 14:35, 14:39, 15:19, 15:34). Among those who experienced this insecurity, as members of a class professionally exposed to it, the noble man was one whose loftiness and serenity of mind enabled him to surmount such difficulties—both preserving his equanimity and keeping to his high purpose.

From what we know about Confucius' experience as an aspiring counsellor to those in power who yet had little success in making himself heard or in finding employment compatible with his own standards for the exercise of power, or from what we learn of him as a teacher of other remnant members of the old aristocracy, whose hereditary functions have become largely usurped by others, we have reason to look beneath the surface of Confucius' seeming platitudes, and find there deep, hard-won convictions achieved in a lifetime of struggle.

We learn too, however, about other attitudes of Confucius that stand in apparent contrast to the Old Testament prophets' frequent indignation against the religious establishment. Confucius is deeply respectful of the ritual traditions that come down from the past. Religious sacrifices, often deprecated by the prophets of Israel, are held in mysterious awe by him. Indeed certain sacrifices seem to Confucius the key to the whole political and social order, and observance of the traditional rites is seen by him as a more effective means of governance than all the laws, punishments and regimentation a ruler might impose on the people (2:3). Reverence is an indispensable virtue of the noble man, who looks up to Heaven's imperatives, the deeds of great men and the words of the sages (16:8). When things go wrong, he does not complain against Heaven or lay the blame on others (14:35). He does not rage like the prophets against all of Israel and a whole generation of men.

Yet Confucius is often classed with other great prophets and spiritual leaders who played a crucial role in the transformation of archaic cultures into traditional civilizations. Arthur Waley linked Confucius to a process in China that moved from an "auguristic-sacrificial" stage to a more humanistic and rational stage of civilization. Karl Jaspers saw Confucius as a key figure in China's "axial age" transition to a high civilizational level. And even allowing for striking differences in the outcome in each case, there are also notable similarities among the major civilizational forces at work.

In China, though Confucius seems so deferential to tradition, it is against a background of obvious challenge to traditional forms and prescriptions in his time. Similarly in India the classical Hindu civilization emerges from a period of intense questioning of the archaic ritual order, expressed in such texts as the *Upanishads,* the early Buddhist *sūtras* and the *Bhagavad Gita.* In each case the authority of the ruling class is deeply implicated in the issue. The Buddha, a prince and representative of the *kshatriya* nobility, rejects temporal rulership and conventional political means as inadequate to deal with the deeper problems of human suffering; the spiritual leadership he now offers is identified by a new concept of nobility as proclaimed in the Four Noble Truths and the Noble Eightfold Path. Likewise in the *Bhagavad Gita,* the *kshatriya* Arjuna is portrayed as calling into the most serious question the concept of duty (*dharma*) that is the raison d'être of the ruling class—a concept that must undergo fundamental reexamination and be reestablished on a new spiritual basis before Arjuna can function again as a warrior and leader of men. Moreover in each case there is a concomitant questioning of the nature, purpose, and ultimate validity of human action. With the Upanishadic seers and the Buddha, it is a question of the efficacy of finite actions for winning release from the karmic order; in the *Gita,* it is a reevaluation of the fruits of action. In Confucius it has to do with the conduct appropriate to the noble man in circumstances wherein not only has he lost much of the power to act but doubts have been raised about the usefulness of taking action on either one's own or others' behalf.

In the preceding chapter we encountered two contrasting views of the role of the prophet in ancient Israel. One identified him as subjecting established society and religion to a most radical critique based on the absolute demands of Yahweh and his exacting standards of justice and righteousness.[1] The other view was of the prophets as "central moral prophets" upholding and perpetuating the highest values of the society.[2] The two views are not incompatible, of course, if we understand the prophet not as an outsider and rebel but rather as an insider—one most dedicated and sensitive to the core values of the society, repeatedly holding his people to account for their fidelity to the values that have sustained their common life. This is true too of Confucius, and it is not surprising that he should do it as a gentleman addressing other gentlemen, for the great transformative movements of human history have generally been led not by disenfranchised proletarians struggling for subsistence but by persons of some education, with the time to reflect upon the adequacy of the existing leadership and the opportunity to question or challenge it.

Reading the *Analects* we become conscious of ourselves as listening in on a conversation among such gentlemen, led by someone respected among them for his learning and character. Of the topics they discuss, the most frequent is that of the *chün-tzu* itself—more frequent by far than any other substantive category, whether of values or social station, more frequent even than such concepts as the Way (*tao*), virtue (*te*), the sage (*sheng jen*), or the king (*wang*). And as we saw in the earlier discussion of the "people" (*min*), even there the discourse is oriented toward the responsibility of the gentleman or the noble man for the people. If we take further into account that Confucius himself is seen as the very model of the noble man, almost everything said by or reported about him in the *Analects* becomes paradigmatic of the *chün-tzu*.

From this we may conclude that the *Analects* as a whole—unstructured, unsystematic, and rambling though this collection of sayings and anecdotes appears to be—has a central focus in the *chün-tzu* and may best be understood from this vantage point. What accounts for its perennial appeal is not that it expounds a philosophy or ideology but that in Confucius it presents such an appealing picture of the noble man.

On this view I propose in what follows to start from what the *Analects* say in direct reference to the *chün-tzu* as such, adding what may be inferred about him in passages that do not explicitly refer to the term; and then consider how the prophetic voice is conditioned in Confucianism by the social and cultural medium, by the fact that the message is borne by a class performing the characteristic roles of the gentleman and fulfilling the lofty vocation of the noble man.

First a matter of terminology. Since I have spoken of the *chün-tzu* as both gentleman and noble man, I must acknowledge that the great majority of references to him in the *Analects* can be understood simply as "gentleman," referring to a class of well-bred persons with gentle ways, impeccable manners, and a developed moral sense. It is only in a minority of cases—though I would say a significant minority—that the *chün-tzu* is cast in the very lofty and self-sacrificing role demanded of the noble man as a leader of others. He is said to be content even in poverty and in humble circumstances that would be considered beneath the dignity and refined tastes of the gentleman (6:9, 15:32, 18:7). No less than the sacrifice of one's life may be called for (15:8). Today we may still think of the gentleman as a model for everyman, in his ordinary conduct of life, a life of gentility, which is true of the *chün-tzu* as well. But above and beyond this the noble man is a model for anyone who might play a leadership role in society, a life of higher responsibilities (19:7). Confucius speaks of the *chün-tzu* in both senses. We are especially reminded of the latter when Confucius draws attention to the more than personal meaning of an action—to its political and social consequences. This happens often; and when it does, something like noblesse oblige is pointed to.

The distinction between gentleman and noble man, though both are combined in the *chün-tzu,* is important because, without it, we may miss or misread the significance of much in the *Analects* that has to do with both inward qualities and outward appearances. Confucius believes it important to uphold high standards of deportment and dress, and a meticulousness in one's use of things, not only for their moral and aesthetic values, but especially for their social implications. Not Confucius alone but virtually all the thinkers of ancient China understood that people aped the leader. But when Confucius speaks of the *chün-tzu* as someone especially careful and restrained, one who is punctilious about not overstepping the bounds of what is right, it is not because he expects ordinary men to exercise the same circumspection or constrain themselves to the same degree, but because those he addresses have a heightened visibility and potentially more far-reaching influence on others, to say nothing of their role in directing others' labors (19:21) and in the distribution of material goods.

In this context it is understandable that Confucius' references to the *chün-tzu* would bring out the qualities that relate him to the people at large, just as references to the *min* most often involve their relation to those above. A basic human empathy is predicated between them, and mutuality or reciprocity of feelings is the implicit basis for all such fiduciary relations (even though the term *shu* itself, empathy or mutuality, occurs only twice in the text). Recognizing this, and accepting his responsibility for initiating the process (8:2), the gentleman / noble man attends to those virtues that generate the appropriate response and corresponding virtue in others: reverence and respect (12:5), filial piety, generosity of heart, and liberality of mind (6:40), consideration for others (5:16), trustworthiness (14:27, 15:18), strength of purpose, courage, determination, and endurance (8:6, 15:2), and in all of these a sense of priority and sequence, especially of the growth process by which certain primary virtues mature into others if properly cultivated (1:2, 19:12).

Given the traditional functions of the *chün-tzu* as members of the ruling elite, it is not surprising that the *Analects* from the start reflect their preoccupation with questions of governance, leadership, and public service. The key to governance, as the maintaining of peace and order (*chih*), is genuine leadership, and the key to the latter is the manifesting of virtues that benefit the people (*te*). Early in the text the underlying issues in governance are stated in terms of the ruler's effect on the people (*min*): "If you lead them by regulations and try to keep them in order by punishments, the people will manage to avoid punishment but will have no sense of shame. If you lead them by virtue and keep them in line by rites, the people will have a sense of shame and regulate themselves" (2:3).

Here virtue (*te*) is a traditional concept for qualities that manifest themselves in benefits to others, but the effect on others most crucial for Confucius is the appeal to their self-respect rather than to fear. At a minimum the consent of the governed is required, but more than that is implied in Confucius' expectation that the people will regulate themselves; there would be some degree of self-government.

Rites are juxtaposed to regulations that rely on force for compliance. Rites have their roots in traditional sacrifices presided over by the head of the ruling house or clan. Together personal virtue and rites combine the moral and religious values underlying traditional society, consensual values contrasted to coercive rule. Each reflects a basic reality of early Chinese life: a kinship system grounded in the agricultural community, with an overlay of military and bureaucratic administration. Ostensibly the enfeoffment system (*feng-chien*) of the Chou embodied familial ties, and the sacrificial rites, participated in by the "feudal" nobility, celebrated the ties and feelings of kinship shared through joint worship of a common ancestor. Apparently Confucius felt the loss of these implicit consensual and fiduciary values associated with a kinship system, in his time increasingly eroded or displaced by the spread of bureaucratic rule, rationalized in explicit impersonal regulations.

In this changed circumstance, Confucius' contribution to the redefining of traditional virtue centered on the concept of humaneness (*jen*). He still talks about virtue as *te,* but humaneness as the perfection of virtue becomes the predominant theme of the *Analects,* in frequency–count outdoing all other concepts by a large margin. As a result, humaneness takes over as the operative personal virtue conjoined to rites and becomes the quality most definitive of Confucius' new understanding of the *chün-tzu* as noble man. One might plausibly interpret this change as taking place under the aegis of Heaven, the sacred canopy legitimating rational, moral rule on a more universal scale. But it also means, humanly speaking, that no government can succeed or be considered legitimate, if it does not rest on an adequate conception of what it means to be fully human; only such a regime can enlist voluntary cooperation and tap the energies of the people.

Two comparisons on the religious level may highlight the shift. One is to the earlier cult of the Lord on High (*shang-ti*), the supreme ancestral deity as the object of reverence in the clan cult of China's rulers, a quasi-anthropomorphic concept as the religious expression of the ruling house's claim to supremacy. This is now overtaken by a more abstract view of Heaven's paternity of all the people. Confucius speaks of Heaven in a personal way as the Supreme Being to whom he is personally answerable in conscience; but as a matter of rite, it is still the Chou ruler, and later emperors, who alone sacrifice to Heaven. Confucius does not speak of this directly in the *Analects,* but it is implied in the saying that "rites, music and punitive expeditions come from the Son of Heaven" (16:2). Later Confucians generally accept this age-old conception of the ruler, with the Son of Heaven serving as the intermediary between Heaven and its people. Humaneness might activate the individual conscience of the noble man, but by rite the one man, the Son of Heaven, still stands at the hierarchical apex of the sacrificial order, performing his duty as chief priest in the Temple of Heaven at the imperial capital. (Even the Korean kings, as good Confucians, recognized this exclusive claim and built themselves an altar of Heaven in Seoul only after declaring their independence of Chinese suzerainty in the late nineteenth century.)

Thus by rite the Son of Heaven stood as the chief priest of the people of all the civilized world. His performance of the sacrifice to Heaven was meant to be the highest ritual act of the supreme pontiff unifying the religious sentiments of all the people. Humaneness, however, became the moral correlate of this as the common denominator among men, the shared moral sentiment exemplified par excellence by the noble man. Indeed so much are the two concepts identified with one another that Confucius says a gentleman who departs from humanity is not worthy to be thought of as a noble man (4:5).

Discussing humanity or humaneness, Confucius often betrays a primary concern for it as the essential quality of the noble man as a leader in society. What he says in the following cannot simply be addressed to the average person, but could be addressed only to one who might find himself in a position of political responsibility: "To be able to practice five virtues everywhere in the world constitutes humanity . . . : courtesy, magnanimity, trustworthiness, diligence, and kindness. He who is courteous is not humiliated, he who is trustworthy wins the people; he who is diligent attains his objective; and he who is kind can get service from the people" (17:6).

One may speculate that this shared humane sentiment of *jen,* implying a common human nature, gained its plausibility from the fact of a relatively homogeneous population, sharing a common culture in the old agricultural heartland of ancient China—a circumstance in some contrast to the ancient Mediterranean civilizations, ethnically, linguistically, and culturally diverse, brought together by sea more than by land, and unified by rather different kinds of imperium, law, and religion.

The key to humaneness is, for Confucius, empathy or mutuality (*shu*). Though rarely mentioned in itself, Confucius speaks of it, along with "being true" (*chung*), as the "one thread that runs through" his teaching (4:15). This is because one comes to understand what it means to be truly human through a process of introspection and self-examination, along with observation and understanding of others. It calls for judging, not oneself as others might see us, but one's actions as others might be affected by them. "What you do not want done to you, do not do to others" (12:2, 15:24). The self-understanding at the heart of *jen,* which some have translated as "human-heartedness," also comes from observing others and learning from this what to emulate in them or avoid in oneself. "When walking in a party of three, I always have teachers. I can take the good qualities of one for imitation, and the bad qualities of the other for correction in myself" (7:21).

As the quintessence of virtue, humaneness is, strictly speaking, open-ended and indefinable; in the full magnitude of its empathetic feeling, *jen* reaches out to all men and even to Heaven itself. Hence Confucius is reluctant to pin it down, or to cite any paragon of such comprehensive virtue. Yet he knows exactly where the cultivation of humaneness begins, and from this standpoint there is nothing vague, elusive, or mysterious about it. It starts with the self in feeling contact with others, following a reliable method—likening oneself to others—that operates through all the virtues, inasmuch as these are bound up with human relations, and all such relations involve some element of reciprocal obligation. "The humane man, desiring to establish himself, seeks to establish others; desiring himself to succeed, he helps others to succeed. To judge others by what one knows of oneself is the method of achieving humanity" (6:28).

Here it is important to understand that reciprocity does not mean an exchange of the same goods or some equivalent return at a given moment in time. Take for example filial piety. One of the earliest references to it is in Confucius' response to a question about the nature of filial piety. No literal translation of Confucius' cryptic answer suffices. Legge's "Parents are anxious lest their children should be sick" (2:6) is about as close as one can get, yet it begs for interpretation. To my mind, the thing most clearly implied is that the root of filial piety lies in the parents' solicitude for the child, and what the child is to do for them comes as a natural response to their prior love, concern, and care. In other words, filial piety is learned from one's parents. Far from being a one-way thing—service to parents—it is intergenerational, an expression of gratitude for the gift of life and an acknowledgment of the family virtues that sustain life from one generation to another.

Note also, however, that it is not a case of one individual's returning to another some exact equivalent in kind. The infant or child cannot make any immediate repayment to the parent; it can begin to reciprocate only as it matures into adulthood, and the parents, declining in old age, become as helpless and dependent on the child as the latter once was on them.

Such an understanding of moral relationships underlies the discussion of filial duty that immediately precedes this passage. After Confucius has defined filial piety laconically as "not being contrary," when someone asks what this means, he says, "When parents are alive, serving them according to what is rite; when dead, mourning for them according to what is rite and sacrificing to them according to what is rite." The key expression here, *i li,* is rendered by Legge as "according to propriety," by Waley as "according to ritual," and by D. C. Lau as "complying with the rites." I translate it as "what is rite" to convey both the objective and subjective aspects of *li*—both the defined form, norm, or measure, and the attitude of mind that makes a response in keeping with it.

Riteness (*li*), as a virtue combining outward form and inner spirit, is referred to by Confucius in three well-known passages in the *Analects*. First there is: "One who is not humane, what has he to do with rites?" (3:3), showing the intimate connection between feeling and form. The second: "Of the things brought about by rites, harmony is the most valuable . . . But to aim at harmony simply because one has learned about harmony, without modulating and measuring it by rites, will not do" (1:12). The third involves a famous dialogue between Confucius and one of his disciples, Tsai Wo, over the observance of the three-year mourning period for one's parents. Tsai Wo thought it too long. Confucius asked him if he could enjoy eating fine food and wearing fine clothes during the mourning period, and when Tsai Wo said he could, Confucius told him to go ahead and do so by all means. But he added that this would not be so of a true gentleman. Later he criticized Tsai Wo for his lack of human feeling. "A child is free from his parents' care only after three years from birth . . . Did not Yü [Tsai Wo] too have the loving care of his parents for three years?" (17:21).

In this case we may note three equally significant points. (1) A proper sentiment is indispensable to the performance of the rite. (2) The true gentleman or noble man is capable of observing the prescribed norm because he is genuinely human; he experiences the appropriate sense of loss. (3) There is a natural reciprocity here measured in terms of the human life-cycle and based on the shared life of the family. It is not a transaction between individuals. The contractual mind is not at work here. Equity is something achieved within the whole context of family life, and as an expression of human feelings in that setting, not on the basis of individual contractual commitments.

The family context of Confucian ethics also is evidenced in Confucius' encounter with a local governor who, boasting of the high level of public morality in his part of the country, cited the son who testified against his father caught stealing a sheep. Confucius countered by saying that in his part of the country the father would shield the son and the son his father (13:18). Here the point lies not in any tangible quid pro quo but in the inviolability of family intimacy. If the most basic human relations cannot be respected and protected within the family where all virtue is nourished, if family members cannot trust one another, the whole fiduciary basis of society stands in jeopardy.

The virtue at issue in this case is forthrightness or straightforwardness (*chih*). It is one of several virtues associated with the gentleman and the latter's living by rites: "Courtesy not in keeping with what is rite becomes laborious bustle; caution not in keeping with what is rite becomes timidity; courage becomes brashness; and forthrightness becomes rudeness" (8:2). Here some translators render *li* as "the rules of propriety" (Legge), or "the prescriptions of ritual" (Waley), while Lau, apparently to avoid overdetermination, translates it as "the spirit of ritual." As before, we have difficulty combining form and spirit in one expression. In the earlier case of mourning for one's parents, Confucius referred to the three-year period as both natural (given the normal term of infancy) and as the generally accepted practice throughout the country. Either way there was something of an objective norm to refer to. In the passage just cited, however, norms become a problem. On the one hand Confucius shows a clear distrust of mere instinct or impulse; some recourse must be had to an external norm or measure. On the other hand it is altogether unlikely that there would be a definite "rule" or "prescription" governing each of the cases cited, and even less so given Confucius' distrust of detailed regulation and legislated controls.

This is one of the deepest problems in the understanding of Confucius and Confucianism. Confucius attaches a crucial importance to rites in the training and cultivation of the gentleman. D. C. Lau points out that in the all-important matter of where the gentleman takes his stand, Confucius says, "Take your stand in the rites" (8:8) and "Unless you study the rites you will not be able to take your stand" (6:13).[3] A key stage in Confucius' self-development was taking a stand at the age of thirty (2:4). He also spoke of rites as a discipline needed to balance the expansive effect of broad learning (6:27). Presumably this implies the acceptance of certain defined limits on oneself. But there is no simple, precise formula for the process of self-definition, and in part it depends on a judgment of others as well as oneself (6:30).

The indicated solution to this dilemma would seem to lie in a prudential judgment involving some reference to past experience, experience of others, established custom, specific ritual texts where available and applicable, and historical examples. The *Tso chuan* chronicle, for instance, is much concerned with what is or is not rite in recorded history. The *chün-tzu* then would need to be well-versed in such matters, and to have developed a practical sense for making balanced judgments in human affairs. And to do this, on any higher level of social responsibility, he would need to be a learned man.

At this point we may note that, if humaneness (*jen*) and riteness (*li*) are the two most prominent virtues of the gentleman/noble man in the *Analects,* learning and knowledge together constitute a third subject of comparable importance. This will not be news to anyone who immediately thinks of Confucians as scholars, but there may be some value in seeing where scholarship fits into the life of the noble man.

By word count, "learning" (*hsüeh*) is the third most discussed topic in the *Analects* among the values identified with the gentle-man. If one includes in the count thematically significant references to *chih,* "knowing" or "learning," together these make up, along with humaneness and rites, the triad of Confucius' chief concerns for the noble man. This is hardly unexpected, given what he says at the start about his delight in learning (1:1) and his early commit-ment to it from the age of fifteen (2:4). This proclivity and com-mitment of his, we soon come to understand, are determinative of his whole course in life. Learning grows as something resolved upon early and, not without difficulty along the way, eventually matures into a rich and self-fulfilling experience for him. It is not, as in some religions, an experience of sudden enlightenment, gnosis or conversion, that immediately changes one's whole per-ception of things, but a task to be worked at, following Heaven's imperative, gradually to shape a life and a self.

Among the many scattered and uncoordinated references to learning, some points emerge clearly. The delight in learning and in sharing it with others is amply confirmed in the rest of the text, so that the disarmingly simple and casual observations of the open-ing lines prove indeed to be keynotes of the *Analects* as a whole. Confucius' eagerness to learn and total dedication to it are everywhere in evidence. A joy for him, as it is also for his favorite disciple Yen Hui (6:12, 11:7), learning also imposes great demands upon him (14:35, 38). At times it is all-consuming, as in its pursuit Confucius forgets to eat and sleep (7:13, 15:30). The reason apart from the pleasure of it is not difficult to find: learning and the pursuit of humaneness go together, and to be fully human, as Heaven's imperative demands of one, is always an unfinished task.[4] The same is true, of course, of one's study of the Way, which is unlimited and forever opens out on new vistas.

Learning is for all because the Way is in all (19:22). All are called to self-understanding and to understanding of others. At first sight this truth may seem to be contradicted in part by Confucius' saying: "In ancient times learning was for one's self; now learning is for the sake of others" (14:24), comparing the latter unfavorably to the former. Here, however, *wei jen,* "for others," is understood in context to mean "for the sake of impressing others or gaining their approval," in contrast to learning that will sustain the inner self even when one is unappreciated by others.

In the latter learning, self-understanding and an active concern for others go hand-in-hand, like companions on the Way. One cannot learn humaneness except by loving others (6:22, 12:12, 12:22, 19:3). This Confucius affirms in repeated declarations that link the pursuit of learning and devotion to teaching (2:11, 7:2, 7:34). He is prepared indeed to instruct anyone willing to make the effort. No one should be excluded from education (14:38) or be discriminated against who is ready and eager to learn (1:14). This implies, of course, a correlative responsibility on the student's part, since for Confucius nothing could be accomplished without the self-motivation and commitment of the student (7:8). Accordingly, how to elicit that motivation also remains a matter of prime concern among later Confucians.

For all this egalitarianism, however, Confucius often makes distinctions of a functional kind among different classes of learners. These must be understood lest one conclude that Confucius is a defender of the gentleman's social privileges (which would, in any case, cast him in a distinctly retrograde, even reactionary role, since such hereditary privileges were already, by his time, becoming a thing of the past). In his day it is a simple fact that most people do not have the means or the leisure to pursue learning, and especially learning of a kind indispensable to the gentleman as a social and political leader. Those who do have the means, and thereby gain access to schooling, should regard education as a trust, to which attaches a responsibility for the care of others. Those who lack the means and the education cannot be expected to bear the same degree of responsibility.

Differentiation of function is, then, a well-established fact of Chinese life, to which certain limitations attach. The uneducated commoner is not equipped to be a leader, even though, as one led, he must never be denied his sense of self-respect. Confucius says that the commander of an army may be captured in battle (and lose his power to lead), but the will of the common man may never be taken from him (9:25). And even the commoner is entitled to some instruction, as we have seen, depending on the functions he is expected to perform.

On the other hand, the gentleman must recognize his own limitations, imposed by his leadership function. No one can do everything or be good in all. Some lead, others follow. Those who lead should devote themselves to the Way (15:31, 17:3). Though people credit Confucius with great versatility, he disavows this on several occasions (7:34, 5:3). He disclaims knowing much about farming and gardening; insists that one who, like himself, is devoted to the study of rites, cannot also be competent in military matters (15:1); and distinguishes the artisan, whose skills are honed in the workshop, from the gentleman who has to pursue broad learning in the world at large (19:7).

While Confucius speaks of certain aspects of learning as specific to the role and responsibilities of the gentleman, others are more generally applicable to all men. Of the former, some attach to the demands of public service—what it will take to fulfill the demanding role of the noble man. Most often Confucius speaks of this as a charge he bears, a commission from Heaven which impels him to unremitting efforts.[5] It is not that he possesses special talents but that he is willing to labor untiringly to fulfill a responsibility others remain oblivious to (16:8, 9; 19:22).

Often when Confucius dwells on the finer points of learning, they are not inherently restricted in their application to any special class, but we sense that they could not have much meaning or relevance except for those with the leisure to engage in scholarship on a high level. Confucius, with his feet always on the ground, says that his learning starts on a lower level but reaches high (14:35). When he talks about the need to combine learning with reflection (2:15, 15:31); to study widely but carefully and with discrimination (2:18, 9:2); to pursue learning broadly but in depth and with a view to integrating everything (6:27, 12:15, 15:3); to be indefatigable in one's questioning (3:15), or when he speaks of studying the past or the rites in depth (3:22, 23; 7:20; 10:13)—in all these respects we judge that he is talking to scholars about the upper reaches of learning.

At other times, regardless of whom he may be addressing, what he says would be applicable to almost anyone—that learning should be about life and what is nearest at hand (7:29, 19:6); that education should enable one to respond to, and accept responsibility for, others (1:7); that learning and practice are inseparable (2:18, 5:14, 11:22); that moral obligations come first and literary or intellectual interests later (1:6); that one must learn from the past in order to deal with the present (2:11, 9:23); that learning helps one to avoid narrowmindedness and rigidity (1:8).

All of these establish learning on a basic human level, but none more so than those passages which reveal Confucius' consciousness of his own doubts and weaknesses as the starting point of learning. Most fundamental and perhaps most memorable of all is his answer to the question of what knowledge consists in: "To know what you do know, and acknowledge what you do not know, is knowledge" (2:17, 5:19). Confucius was persistently modest about his own learning (5:9, 9:8, 13:3, 19:5), conscious of his faults and determined to correct them (5:15, 7:3, 7:31). If then he set much store by learning, and indeed reveled in it, one understands that this celebration of learning is grounded in a profound awareness of human limits and the need to accept such limits as the precondition for the cultivation of man's talents, the development of human potentialities or the enlargement of human knowledge. Such an awareness informs almost every word in the *Analects,* because it constrains Confucius' use of language and demands that words be employed with the greatest precision to state exactly what one does and does not know (4:22, 24; 7:28; 13:3, 14:20, 27). It is this awareness that both allows for a prophetic voice in Confucianism, as a critique of human weakness and error, and also constrains that voice to speak without self-righteousness or exaggeration.

Finally, to bring this discussion of learning back to the other two main concerns of the noble man, moral virtue and rites, one should note that for Confucius learning is as integral to the cultivation of virtue as are rites. This is apparent in the parallel between the following passages:

> When one loves humaneness without loving learning, it is corrupted into foolishness
> When one loves sagacity without loving learning, it is corrupted into deviousness
> When one loves trustworthiness without loving learning, it is corrupted into blind faith
> When one loves forthrightness without loving learning, it is corrupted into rudeness
> When one loves courage without loving learning, it is corrupted into truculence. (17:8)

Compare this to what he has said about rites: "Courtesy not in keeping with what is rite becomes laborious bustle; caution not in keeping with what is rite becomes brashness; forthrightness not in keeping with what is rite becomes rudeness" (8:2). As seen by Confucius, moral feelings or impulses alone, unguided by learning and untempered by the observance of rites as the norms of past experience, were unlikely to hit the mark in practice.

For Confucius it was more than a matter of being literate, literary, or erudite, though the Confucian scholar's skills, his technical virtuosity in these respects, became crucial to his historically important role as civil servant or mandarin. Whatever might be adjudged the practical success, if any, of the Confucian in later times, learning for him could never be just a business, any more than expertise in ritual could be, though each had its attractiveness to China's imperial rulers. For Confucius, humaneness, riteness, and learning were integral parts of a single ethos.

To Confucius the carrying on of a civilized tradition, a culture (*wen*), though no doubt originating in oral tradition, was increasingly identified with literate discourse and the preservation of records and standards. His mission in life consisted in perpetuating this legacy, "this culture" (*ssu wen*) (9:5), no less than in public service. We need not repeat here many sayings of his that confirm this mission. We have seen that one of the rare claims Confucius makes for himself is that he yields to no one in his love of learning (5:28). To this learning of the Way he devoted himself untiringly, regardless of what other disappointments he suffered in life (8:13, 14:38, 18:7). What made life worth the struggle, and even made his own survival a matter of urgent importance, was his dedication to preserving the best that had been achieved by humankind in the realization of the Way (9:5, 18:6).

Though Confucius did not himself define the canon of Confucian classics, there can be no real doubt that he did much to shape it, for the contents of the canon reflect the same dominant concerns of the gentleman as those given in the *Analects:* human governance, human rites, and the expression of human sentiments in forms much like our "humanities"—the classic subjects Confucius discoursed upon according to the *Analects* (7:18, 7:24): the Odes, the Documents of History, the Rites.

A moral tone is evident but should not be exaggerated as moralistic. Confucius spoke of *wen,* letters in the broadest sense, as precisely that, "broadening," in contrast to the limiting or constraining function of rites (9:11). Letters opened up a range of experience and revealed variegated patterns of aesthetic refinement; rites set bounds, imposed restraint.

For Confucius these opposing values were both necessary and complementary. To accept them as such was to accept human life, at its best, as lived in the midst of such tensions, trying to strike the Mean. Much of the *Analects* has to do with this balancing act and art.

If we say that the gentleman was an artist of life, it means that he could be something of an aesthete but never a dilettante. Confucius had his moments of literary and aesthetic enjoyment, but they came after the discharge of moral duties and social responsibilities (1:6). Even if rites exerted moral constraints, however, they were almost always linked to music and dance, and had this in common with arts and letters: they gave expression to human feelings and moral sentiments, refinement to the raw substance of human emotion. Together they brought human intelligence and sensibility to bear on life, imposing a certain order or pattern on things that was in keeping with the life-engendering and nourishing power of the Way, just as ditches, dikes, and furrows put man's mark on the native soil of China.

Confucian gentlemen accepted this present world as the one in which the Way was to be realized, by actions that would also transform it. One could not act as if the form of things were insignificant or ephemeral, or formalism "a mere formality." Formalism gave expression to the Way, substantiated it, impressed on things a defined set of values.

Reverence for Heaven, to Confucius, meant reverence for life, caring for the things of this world as Heaven's offspring. If the Confucian "lifestyle" seemed unduly cautious and constrained, and this set Confucians apart from ordinary men, it was because they cared more for life. And if the critics of the Confucians found their style fussy, pedantic, or irritating, at least the Confucians did not let standards go by default.

In Confucius' mind such a conscientious, indeed scrupulous, attitude in all areas of life need not leave one fretful and anxiety-ridden (7:37, 12:4). The gentleman who examined his conscience and found it clear could deal confidently with the world and not look for others to blame (15:21). In time he might even expect to achieve the ease and freedom of Confucius at the age of seventy, who could "follow his heart's desire without transgressing" (2:4).

Historically, it is true, things were not that easy. One so committed to the rites of civilization—shaping and ordering things in the way that humans shaped and ordered the land in agriculture—understood the need for adapting to the contours of place and time, climate and season. Confucius recognized that ages differed and rites (institutions) changed, as he believed they had from the Hsia to the Shang and to the Chou dynasties (2:23). He chose to follow the rites of Chou because, he said, the Chou were "nearest" in time and circumstance and had learned something from their predecessors (3:14). Learning from the past was important in two ways: upholding life-sustaining hopes and ideals, and learning from past experience. Confucius struggled to sustain his hopes for a restoration of the Chou system. His successors, having adapted his ideal models as best they could to the realities of one age, found each new age a new challenge. Adaptations made in one could prove unacceptable or unworkable in the next.

In the *Analects* the rites of the gentleman had been interiorized to some degree as riteness in the noble man and could be appropriated by anyone raising himself to that level. Still to the extent that they remained a form or formality as codified in the ritual texts, the rites were a vestige of the old aristocratic order, not easily assimilated, if at all, by the common people. By Sung times the Neo-Confucians were strongly conscious that the classical rites worked for almost nobody, the common people followed "vulgar popular customs," disgusting and corrupt in the eyes of the educated, while even the latter found the classic rites too elaborate, expensive, and anachronistic to suit their more limited means and circumstances. Several attempts were made to redefine and simplify the rites, most notably by Ssu-ma Kuang and Chu Hsi. Chu's *Family Ritual,* the most influential of such formulations, was meant to be practicable within the means of poor scholars like himself, and even contribute to the uplift of the common people, as part of the "renewal of the people." Even so it covered only a small area of the social and political ground of the classic rites, and was practiced only among the relatively educated elite or near-elite. Most Confucians continued to deplore the prevalence of corrupt customs among the common people.

Take for another example an institution of government such as was formerly embraced in the sphere of rites: the incorporation of the Confucian humanities in the imperial civil service system. What impressed all of East Asia as a great achievement in the T'ang examination system proved unacceptable to Confucian reformers in the Sung, who felt that moral substance had been sacrificed to literary style or mere rote-learning. It cannot be said that the successive reforms of the Sung, Yüan, and Ming fully solved this problem, but they did produce a remarkably stable system, only to have this become a major obstacle to progress in the nineteenth century, and be completely swept away in the early twentieth.

Given the Confucians' strong affirmation of life and commitment to the value of human experience, it was not possible for the *chün-tzu* to perform his prophetic functions with the same sharp and sweeping condemnations of Heaven's people as did the Old Testament prophets of God's people. Nor, for that matter, could they offer the prospect of a redemption so far removed from existing realities. But, just the same, they were caught up in a struggle no less demanding.

For if Confucius, against all apparent odds, insisted that he had to change things in order to make the Way prevail, he was no less burdened than the prophets with his Heaven-ordained mission. It was indeed a double burden—to preserve all he could of the human culture by which sages and worthies had brought the Way into the world, while also transforming everything worldly that did not conform to that Way.

If we understand "this culture" (*ssu wen*) as the best approximation yet achieved of that Way, and accept too the Confucian's responsibility to conserve and extend that culture by incorporating it—giving it body, form, pattern, and meaning—in each age, we cannot underestimate the challenge it presented to the noblest of Confucian gentlemen.

In every age the effort was to be made again to realize this ideal. In each a new critique had to be offered of all that had gone before. Ridiculed for their antique ways, for their stubborn adherence to ancient models, for keeping to quaint habits that bespoke their fidelity to tradition, for holding to a dedicated simplicity and frugality that seemed utterly to belie their enjoyment of life and refined tastes, the Confucians nevertheless had to summon up the courage and energy to struggle with a world they sought to transform.

The problem would only intensify with the passage of time. Even though the true dimensions of the struggle would not be recognized by a modern world with the prospect of unlimited progress before it, undisposed to see anything in this past but stagnation and resistance to change, a larger, less jaundiced view would see some Confucian success along with repeated failures. But few modern critics would notice how often seeming failures were the by-products of veritable successes, or how often success achieved in one area seems to have been achieved at the cost of neglect in another. Toward the end of the imperial age, for instance, Confucian classical scholarship attained unprecedented heights in the so-called Han learning of the Ch'ing dynasty, only to be faulted by Neo-Confucian prophets (Fang Tung-shu in the nineteenth century and T'ang Chun-i in the twentieth) for its neglect of moral issues and moral philosophy.

Just one more question to conclude this reflection on the noble man as seen in the *Analects*. Confucius identifies him with three main values: humaneness, rites, and letters (or scholarship). In this century Confucianism has been successfully buried (in the May Fourth Movement); disinterred and either desecrated or made a museum piece (during the Mao era); and now revived as a live subject of sociological study (for example, the East Asian work ethic) or as a moral philosophy. Confucian humaneness has become easy to sell, if not to practice. The noble man himself may well find a place in academia or the new world bureaucracy. Rites or riteness, however, seems to have no advocates in the modern world. Indeed a case could be made that the rites have been in decline, if not moribund, for centuries. What does this tell us about the viability of Confucianism, supported by only two feet, moral philosophy and scholarship, of the original tripod?

But if something is missing from the original Confucian vision in this respect, is it not also what is most lacking in the modern world: social forms and institutions supportive of both civility and civilization? What else can salvage something from the emotional wreckage and environmental damage of the industrial age, and restore mankind to "what is rite"—a proper relationship among Heaven, earth, and man? Perhaps the trouble with Confucianism is also the trouble with the modern world.

3

Imperial Sages
and Confucian
Noble Men

AFTER MENCIUS had so asserted the dignity and independence of
the minister, Chinese rulers who still claimed the authority, omni-
science, and omnicompetence of the sage could not expect that
claim to go undisputed by the Confucians. Though officially unrecognized and politically powerless against the highly organized
and efficient Legalists, who succeeded in conquering, unifying, and
reorganizing China in the third century B.C., the Confucians' influence was nonetheless acknowledged indirectly by the Legalist
prime minister of the Ch'in empire, Li Ssu, when he called for the
burning of the Confucian books and directed those seeking an education to get their instruction from official sources, not from im-
practically bookish and yet ideologically troublesome Confucians
who "harp on the past to injure the present." In a memorial to the
throne, Li accused the Confucians of promoting open criticism and
expressing views contrary to the ruler's. He recommended that
"those who dare to talk to each other about the *Book of Odes* and
Book of Documents should be executed and their bodies exposed in
the marketplace. Anyone referring to the past to criticize the present should, with all the members of his family, be put to death."[1]

Even allowing for the alacrity with which Legalists of Li Ssu's
stripe resorted to extreme punishments, one may infer from the
drastic measures he proposed that, to his mind, the Confucians represented a veritable threat. Despite their antiquarian and pedantic
ways, Li speaks of them as having influence with the multitudes and
stirring up opposition. This, in his eyes, cannot but jeopardize the
authority of the emperor, who, Li says, has reunified the empire
after its earlier disintegration, brought all thought and activity

under his own direction and dictation, and "established for himself a position of sole supremacy."[2]

Apparently these Confucian traditionalists, punctilious pedants though they appeared to be, were more than just gentlemen scholars and courtly ritualists in the Weberian mold. They were noble men of the type Mencius called for: critics whose protest could be quite telling. Plainly, if self-proclaimed sage-rulers meant trouble for the Confucians, the trouble with Confucianism for the ruler could be found in the noble man.

The Trouble with Confucian Scholarship

When Confucianism finally emerged as a state-sanctioned teaching, with official status at court, it was in the reign of the great Emperor Wu of the Han dynasty. Tung Chung-shu (179?–104? B.C.), a leading scholarly authority on the *Spring and Autumn Annals* who might best be described as a philosopher of history, was also a leading figure at court, recognized as such by the Confucian scholars of his time and especially respected for his character and integrity. Tung had definite views about political and economic reform, and in advocating them recalled both the ideal order of the sage-kings and the principles of Mencius. Arguably, as a proponent of such ideals and a critic of the Ch'in-Han system, he could be considered a political prophet, but that may be going too far. Though he believed in the equalization of land-holding and hoped for a return to the ancient well-fields system advocated by Mencius, in the end Tung felt the need to compromise with the established order, settling in his own mind for a moderate limitation on land-holding rather than insisting on radical redistribution. By Mencius' criteria, as conscientious statesman and reformer Tung might well merit the title "noble man," but as the embodiment equally of Confucian courage and prudence, and as quintessential classicist and philosopher, he was unlikely to press his case with the shrill or stern voice of the prophet.

Officially Tung and his Han Confucian colleagues were honored at court as erudite scholars and professors of the classics, but as Emperor Wu turned increasingly to professional bureaucrats— technicians and fiscal experts identified with Legalist methods—for the management of his finances and imposition of expanded state controls over the economy, the Confucians rose in opposition. Things came to a head in 81 B.C. with the historic Debate on Salt and Iron (so called because it centered on the issue of state monopolies over these essential resources).

Significantly, however, the debate departed from the familiar Confucian-Legalist contest over the primacy of state power. Rather than assuming state supremacy as the highest value (as had Li Ssu earlier), here the supposedly "Legalist" types argued that their policies primarily served the people's interest—that is, promoted the public development, fair distribution, or conservation of limited resources, instead of allowing uncontrolled private exploitation. Confucian spokesmen, basing themselves on Mencius, contended that this economic function was better left in the hands of the "people" themselves, meaning it was better left in private hands (what today might be called "free enterprise") than those of the state bureaucracy.

Which party then could really speak for the "people's" interest? We may not be in a position to arrive at a definitive judgment, given the inchoate nature of popular sentiments in those times, but two points are worth noting. The first is that in the debate itself, the government experts belittled the Confucians as poor, threadbare, impractical scholars, incompetent to handle their own affairs, let alone those of the state. The Imperial Secretary is recorded as saying of the Confucians: "See them now present us with nothing and consider it substance, with emptiness and call it plenty! In their coarse gowns and cheap sandals they walk gravely along, sunk in meditation as though they had lost something. These are not men who can do great deeds and win fame. They do not even rise above the vulgar masses!"[3]

This diatribe perpetuates the long-standing reputation of the Confucians as straitlaced but impecunious scholars, not at all men of the world or well-adjusted to it, but almost misfits. Here we need a word for them that conveys their sense of mission and disciplined, even if arcane, lifestyle. "Academician" (especially when thought of in cap and gown, or in the pejorative sense, as when an issue is dismissed as "purely academic") might do and is certainly closer to it than "preacher" or "prophet," yet Confucians professed a greater dedication to defined moral values than we customarily associate with the "value-free" academics of today. In any case the distinguishing characteristic of the Confucians, in the eyes of their contemporaries, is their cultural commitment, idealistic dedication, and shared values as a company of scholars, rather than any economic class interest, proprietary power, party organization, or entrenched social position.

The second point worth noting is that the great debate was won ostensibly by the Confucians but practically by elements, including eunuchs, in the inner court surrounding the imperial family, who exploited the rhetoric of the Confucians to advance their own interests in a power struggle with the dominant faction in the regular state (or civil) administration. Once in power themselves, the inner palace group largely dispensed with the Confucians and made their own compromise with the established revenue-raising agencies, which, though somewhat curbed, remained essentially intact.[4]

The actual weakness of the Confucians, then, seems to have lain not in a failure of advocacy, but in their indisposition or inability to establish any power base of their own. They could serve important functions for the bureaucratic state by virtue of their literacy, their knowledge of history and ritual, and their high-minded ethos, but except on rare, momentary occasions, they faced the state, and whoever controlled it in the imperial court, as individual scholars unsupported by an organized party or active constituency. It is this institutional weakness, highly dependent condition, and extreme insecurity in their individual tenure of office (correctly diagnosed by Weber), and not any failure to uphold transcendent values (since they were hard enough on, demanding enough of, themselves), that marked the Confucians as *ju* ("softies") in the politics of imperial China.

In the T'ang dynasty, with the Confucian classics and literary composition installed as fixtures in the civil service examination, the literati acquired an even stronger identification with dynastic institutions, but did not succeed in overcoming this crucial handicap. As Confucian scholar-officials they remained exposed to the vicissitudes of a system that took advantage of their disciplined talents while keeping them in a condition of extreme dependency and grave insecurity—though whether in servitude or not is another matter.

The pathos of this situation for the conscientious Confucian—mindful of Confucius' persistent sense of mission, and refusing, in the face of extreme difficulties, either to give up or give in—has been touchingly expressed by the great T'ang poet, Tu Fu (712–770), as he struggled to carry on his own political vocation when out of office, and almost had to go begging for help from friends in different parts of the country. Here are two poems written in his last years:

Early Sailing

Every quest is preceded by a hundred scruples; Confucianism is indeed one of my troubles. And yet, because of it, I have many friends. And despite my age I have continued to travel . . . Wise men of ancient times would not expose themselves to any chance of danger; why should we hurry now at the risk of our lives? . . .

Having come a long, hard way to be a guest; One can make few appeals without injuring one's self-respect. Among the ancients, there were good men who refused to compromise and starved to death; There were able men who humored the world and received rich gifts. These are mutually exclusive examples; The trouble with me is that I want to follow them both![5]

On the River

On the river, every day these heavy rains—
bleak, bleak, autumn in Ching-ch'u!
High winds strip the leaves from the trees;
through the long night I hug my fur robe.
I recall my official record, keep looking in the mirror,
recall my comings and goings, leaning alone in an upper
    room.
In these perilous times I long to serve my sovereign—
old and feeble as I am, I can't stop thinking of it![6]

So much for the noble man in T'ang China. Politically Tu Fu was a failure, but in its candor his poetry reveals the pathos of the all-too-human noble man dedicated to high ideals.

The Sung saw increasing centralization of power in the imperial state, and Confucian ministers sought to offset or balance this further concentration of power in the hands of the ruler by strengthening their own position at court. One such effort consisted of lectures on the "Learning of the Emperors and Kings" (*Ti-wang chih hsüeh*) or, for short, the "Learning of the Emperors" (*Ti-hsüeh*). Here the basic idea was that the sage-kings of ancient times had been advised by sage-ministers, and what emperors needed to learn in the present was to follow the example of the sages in this respect—to keep wise, learned, and straight-talking Confucians as confidants and mentors.

As expressed in lectures to the emperor or crown prince, and as put in writing by leading Neo-Confucian scholars, the content of this instruction celebrated wise rulers who listened to wise ministers, or held up as object-lessons rulers who listened to unworthy ministers and came to ruin. Learning from this the ruler should listen to criticism and, to be receptive to it, he must cultivate habits of mind that would sensitize him to the moral and political issues involved. "Rectifying the mind and making one's intentions sincere" became a central theme.

One of the Confucians who gave such lectures, Ch'eng I, took up Mencius' prophetic role with great seriousness. He insisted that Confucian ministers who counselled the ruler be treated with the greatest respect, and thought it an indignity that he should actually have to apply for an official stipend, as if he were a mere hireling.

When he lectured to the emperor in the early Yüan-yu period (1086–1093), Ch'eng I insisted on upholding the dignity of the teacher as a paramount value, even if it meant showing less respect for the ruler than was customary. He became well-known for his sternness in admonishing the emperor, who it is reported, felt great dread of him. When someone suggested to Ch'eng I that he should be less overbearing and follow rather the example of more respectful officials senior to him in age and position, Ch'eng demurred. Insisting that the teacher's responsibility overrode all considerations of rank, he said, "I am a commoner. As the teacher of the Emperor, I must maintain my self-respect and dignity."[7]

Chu Hsi (1130–1200) incorporated a key formulation of this theme in his preface to the *Mean* (*Chung-yung*). Following Ch'eng I, Chu asserted that the essential method of rulership had been passed down by the sage-kings in a sixteen-character formula:

"The mind of man is precarious, the mind of the Way is subtle. Be refined, be single-minded. Hold fast the Mean." This cryptic message, drawn from a text claiming the ancient authority of the classic *Book of Documents,* was interpreted to mean that the mind of man is precariously poised between legitimate desires and good intentions, on the one hand, and selfish, potentially destructive ones, on the other. The ruler, especially in view of his great power and the effect of his decisions on others, had to be especially careful to discriminate between worthy and unworthy intentions, hold single-mindedly to correct principles, and be balanced in his judgments. Chu Hsi called this the message and method of the mind for the ruler (*hsin-fa*).

Chu also identified this message as the essence of the sages' teaching, the secret of which had been lost from the time of Mencius to that of the Ch'eng brothers in the eleventh century. The written record being so fragmentary and obscure, it was only the extraordinary insight and deep concern of the Ch'engs that allowed them to recover and repossess the essential import of this "message of the mind." There being no direct line of transmission from Mencius, only a kind of prophetic inspiration could bring the message to light and to the attention of rulers.

This is not the place to review the subsequent efforts of Neo-Confucian ministers to propagate this message.[8] For present purposes I cite, by contrast, the appropriation of Neo-Confucian teachings by two powerful imperial sages of the early Ming, who typify the relationship between Confucianism and the dynastic system. The founder Ming T'ai-tsu (1368–1399) confirmed the important role of Confucian scholars in the civil bureaucracy by resuming the civil service examinations, based on the Neo-Confucian curriculum of Chu Hsi, which the Yüan dynasty had first adopted in 1313–1315. Indeed T'ai-tsu strengthened the system by allowing almost no access to office except through this meritocratic route. On the other hand, as a man of humble origins and largely self-educated, he showed considerable distaste for Neo-Confucian scholarship and philosophy as such, making plain his preference for men who combined literacy with practical learning, in contrast to Neo-Confucians distinguished by their literary refinement and philosophical sophistication.

A ruthless despot in dealing with ministers he came to distrust,

T'ai-tsu in his megalomania abolished the prime ministership in order to centralize and concentrate all executive power in his own hands; simultaneously, through a series of imperial pronouncements and directives, he exercised supreme ideological authority in matters of moral, social, and political doctrine.[9] It will not surprise my readers to learn that, even while giving the Neo-Confucian Four Books their greatest prominence in education and the examination system, T'ai-tsu saw to it that the text of Mencius was expurgated so as to remove from it passages considered contumacious or subversive of the ruler's supreme authority.

The third Ming emperor, Ch'eng-tsu (reigned 1402–1425), a usurper of the throne, was no less assertive of imperial authority and ruthless in dealing with his ministers. To enhance his legitimacy, he made a great show of patronizing Neo-Confucianism, even though outspoken ministers (loyal in the Confucian sense of giving the ruler honest advice) were subjected by him to terror, imprisonment, torture, and death. At Ch'eng-tsu's direction a massive compilation of Neo-Confucian texts was printed and officially promulgated in 1415, to become the authoritative canon of Neo-Confucian teaching for centuries—in Ming China, in Yi dynasty Korea, and Tokugawa Japan. Ch'eng-tsu also compiled and had published in his own name a guide to self-cultivation and mind control identified as "The Message of the Mind in the Sages' Learning" (*Sheng-hsüeh hsin-fa*). This later work had far less influence, no doubt because Ch'eng-tsu's presumptuousness in claiming to speak as a sage did not impress later generations of scholars. On the contrary the Ch'ing dynasty editors of the Imperial Manuscript Library Catalogue later castigated Ch'eng-tsu for this presumption, when more properly he should, as the ruling authority, simply have authorized and given his imprimatur to what more competent scholarly authorities had been asked to prepare. As I have summarized this scholarly judgment elsewhere, the editors said of Ch'eng-tsu that "he showed no sense of modesty or shame." They note the blood spilled in his rise to power, the harshness of his rule, the many who suffered unjustly from his arbitrary decrees and excessive punishments, all in contrast to the benevolent professions of the work in question. They conclude: "Men of later generations would not be taken in by this hypocrisy."[10]

There is great irony in the Ming situation, considering that it was in a real sense *the* first full "Neo-Confucian" period—the first in which nearly all educated men, from the beginning, received their intellectual and moral formation through Neo-Confucian teachers and a Neo-Confucian curriculum. Neo-Confucian texts served as the basis for state examinations, and even Ming emperors (whether as crown princes or after) were constantly lectured to by Neo-Confucian mentors. Yet by the almost unanimous verdict of historians, Ming rule has been adjudged the ultimate extreme in Chinese despotism. Lest one dismiss this as just a Western judgment, prejudiced perhaps by ignorance, cultural preconceptions, or a predisposition to denigrate the Chinese, it must be said that Chinese scholars themselves, by the end of the Ming, had already arrived at this condemnation.

Modern writers have sometimes explained this ironic outcome as an indication that Neo-Confucianism itself was to blame, that it bore the seeds of such despotism in its own "dogmatism" and authoritarian ways. Still others who find Neo-Confucians to blame do so for almost opposite reasons, citing their impractical idealism, naive optimism, and simple moralistic approach to politics that was altogether incapable of coping with the economic complications and Byzantine complexities of imperial politics.[11] This latter explanation may be closer to the truth than the former, in that Neo-Confucian self-cultivation—the heart of its educational doctrine—put such heavy emphasis on the power of the individual moral will to master any situation. Thus when his ministers and mentors, with all of the best intentions, seemed to lodge in the emperor ultimate responsibility for whatever went wrong in the world as the very necessary implication and consequence of imperial claims to absolute authority, it was an unbearable moral burden for the man at the top—"the one man"—to bear. There are signs that Ming rulers developed deep psychological resistance to this unequal situation, resented being lectured to in such terms, and in some cases refused even to meet with their Neo-Confucian ministers for long periods of time—even years on end.[12] A strikingly similar syndrome appeared in Yi dynasty Korea, where the same system of Neo-Confucian instruction for the ruler was adopted, sometimes with incongruous results.[13]

If there is any situation to which Thomas Metzger's theory—

that Neo-Confucian doctrine (rather than the traditional Confucian dilemma) placed its adherents in a kind of ultimate "predicament"[14]—is particularly applicable, it is certainly here, yet more applicable to the ruler than to the minister, since the latter could ease his Confucian conscience and extricate himself from this psychological dilemma by noting the disjointed times and likening himself to Confucius' noble man, who "remains unsoured even though unrecognized." He might take the ritual blame at court, but the scholar-minister could console himself with the thought that Confucius, too, had had to struggle on in adverse circumstances, and political frustration was not necessarily a sign of moral failure. The ruler, however, had no one to blame but himself. Though the historical situations are not quite parallel, his "predicament" bears some resemblance to that of the emperor of Japan at the end of World War II, when he was glad to renounce any claims to "divinity," since he found it a rather "uncomfortable" position to be in, as well as an impossible role to fulfill.[15]

Neo-Confucian historians, however, saw more in this situation than simply a test of individual moral wills. Huang Tsung-hsi (1610–1695) and Ku Yen-wu (1613–1682) wrote searching critiques of the dynastic institutions which placed so many conscientious Confucians in seemingly hopeless predicaments—situations wherein even the most extraordinary heroism and self-sacrifice could do little to overcome the inherent defects in such a flawed system, or cope, as I said at the outset, with the "ungovernability of imperial rule" by supposed sage-emperors. Reassessing the prime Neo-Confucian political dictum that self-cultivation (self-discipline) was the key to the governance of men (*hsiu-chi chih-jen*), Huang, as I pointed out in *The Liberal Tradition in China,* insisted that without the right laws and institutions it was almost impossible for the individual to do right.[16] Only with proper laws could men be properly governed (*Yu chih fa erh hou yu chih jen*). Nor were these wholly exceptional views, expressed only by a few nonconformists. There is much evidence, increasingly being brought to light in recent studies, that such views were indeed shared among seventeenth-century scholars, deeply shaken by the catastrophic consequences of Ming despotism in both its violent excesses and dire deficiencies.[17]

Thus, as we leave the Ming dynasty, we still face in seventeenth-century China the same long-standing tension between Confucian ideals and Chinese imperial rule, between the noble man and the sage-emperor. This may well leave one with the strong impression of a stand-off between the two, and that would not be wrong. But other Confucian prophets spoke to the matter in ways that may shed more light on this apparent stalemate. Western history exhibits more motion, development, and seeming progress than does Chinese, but if we can learn to look at things in a Chinese perspective, with something of the patience and longanimity of the Chinese, it may stand us in good stead. For the problem is still with us today, in only slightly altered form. No modern rush to judgment, no urge for a quick solution, has made it yield to our wishes or produced a deus ex machina from the Goddess of Democracy at T'ien-an men. With this thought, then, that we too must learn to live with the problem, I propose to extend the discussion into the nineteenth century, when this long-standing stalemate is broken open by violent intrusion from the West.

4

Autocracy and the Prophetic Message in Orthodox Neo-Confucianism

IN *THE LIBERAL TRADITION IN CHINA* I chose to start not deductively from a preconceived Western definition of liberalism, but inductively from examples in Sung and Ming Neo-Confucianism that might reasonably be thought "liberal" by ordinary understandings of the term. Together they represented, for me, a distinctive Chinese phenomenon, expressed in Chinese terms and to be understood in a Chinese context—by no means the exact equivalent of modern Western "liberalism." On this basis various forms of "liberal" criticism or protest in China might be defined positively, in terms of the ideal standards they tried to uphold, but also negatively, by what they opposed. Thus Chinese liberalism was conditioned significantly by Chinese despotism, as it was also delimited by it. Acts of heroic protest, such as Fang Hsiao-ju's self-sacrifice in resisting the usurpation and oppression of Ming Ch'eng-tsu (the Yung-lo emperor 1403–1424) or Hai Jui's excoriation of Ming Shih-tsung's incompetence and corruption in the Chia-ching period (1522–1566), would not have been evoked had not the consciences of these Confucian ministers first been aroused and then put to the ultimate test by their rulers. For Confucius, self-sacrifice was nothing to be sought after; endurance and survival were preferable to martyrdom (*Analects* 15:7). Thus there might have been fewer Confucian martyrs had it not been for Chinese despots who first called noble men forth to serve and then tried to silence them when they could not be coopted.

But if autocracy in China both bred and stunted its own kind of liberal protest, it is noteworthy that these critics, prophets, and martyrs mostly came from among the Confucians—and in the cases just cited, specifically from the ranks of orthodox Neo-Confucians—not from among Buddhists or Taoists. The latter were, as we say, out of it, not engaged in the kind of struggle religion waged against Caesar in the West. In this respect Confucianism—not a teaching usually considered "religious"—performed the critical function Max Weber assigned to religion as the effective bearer of compelling, transcendental values in vital tension with the world, while Buddhism and Taoism, normally considered "religions," rarely did so.

Robert Bellah has said that "every religion tries to remake the world in its own image, but is always to some extent remade in the image of the world." [1] This is true of Confucianism, and of Taoism and Buddhism as well, but how they are remade reflects also the extent to which, and the manner in which, they themselves actually *try* to remake the world. In the case we have here, it is a question whether Buddhism and Taoism even *tried* in the way Confucianism did.

No doubt some readers, recalling certain messianic movements and peasant rebellions in China of Buddhist or Taoist inspiration, will ask if these religions did not represent some revolutionary potential. Professor Eisenstadt, for his part, would explain these movements as failing in political effectiveness or transformative power mainly on account of extrinsic factors—the ability of the state to deny them any purchase on central ground, to hold them off and contain them at the periphery of power. Thus marginalized, they could exert no leverage on the political world. [2]

However this may be, it is also true that the state rarely had to contend with more than an ephemeral challenge from these religions, inasmuch as they failed to generate any systematic political doctrine, ideology of power, or set of principles on which to ground an organizational ethos. For them the failure to mount a serious challenge at the center was more a matter of default than of actual defeat or containment. In the West, Stalin is said to have dismissed Roman Catholicism as a force to be reckoned with by asking, "How many divisions has the Pope?" In China, Buddhist and Taoist messianism, even though capable of rousing rebellions, could be discounted as viable political forces by asking the contrasting question, "Where is their alternative to the civil service?"

If, then, we see both the imperial bureaucratic tradition and its liberal critics in Ming China as somehow linked through their association with Neo-Confucianism, what, we may ask, later became of this uneasy combination and troubled union? Did Confucian scholars cease to offer a challenge to the state in the succeeding Manchu dynasty? Did the prophetic function lapse with the rise of a new and more efficient autocracy? Was orthodox Neo-Confucianism as reaffirmed by the Ch'ing somehow decontaminated, rendered sterile of such dissent and protest? And if this vital challenge was missing, did Chinese civilization, without it, find its further growth stalemated, lacking the stimulus of prophecy and the goad of criticism? Did China, for want of such prodding, lapse into inertia or fall into a torpor from which it could be roused only by the more dynamic, transformative power of the West?

In at least partial answer to these questions, I should like here to offer two examples, drawn from the heart of Neo-Confucian orthodoxy, which demonstrate that the essential tension between ideal and reality was sustained, and that, at least in the realm of ideas, there remained the possibility of a radical critique of the established order being generated from within the tradition, drawing on the same concepts, transcendent values and prophetic utterance as in the past. Moreover both of the scholars I shall cite, though largely neglected in histories of Ch'ing thought, were recognized in their own time as leading spokesmen for orthodox Neo-Confucianism, not just minor exceptions or dissidents without real influence. The failure of modern scholarship to take them into account when theorizing about Neo-Confucianism shows how the modern mentality can wear blinders as narrowing as those of the supposedly blind orthodoxies of the past.

Lü Liu-liang as an Orthodox Neo-Confucian Radical

In the early years of this century Lü Liu-liang (1629–1683) was known primarily as a Ming loyalist who refused to serve the Manchus and yet was also a leader in the revival of Chu Hsi's teachings in the early Ch'ing period. There was nothing implausible about this combination of Neo-Confucian orthodoxy and dynastic loyalty, but in the revolutionary ferment at the end of the Ch'ing period it is understandable that Lü's anti-Manchu sentiments would have attracted more attention than his Neo-Confucian convictions. The latter, however, included radical political ideas akin to those of his better-known contemporary Huang Tsung-hsi (1610–1695).[3]

Lü's views, parallel to Huang's at many points, are embedded in his recorded dialogues and commentaries on the Four Books, widely circulated in his own day on account of their usefulness to examination candidates, but later suppressed by the Yung-cheng emperor as a consequence of the Tseng Ching case (1728). What is particularly intriguing about Lü is that he had resigned as an official stipendiary, refusing to serve under the Manchus, but made a living writing, printing, and selling model examination essays, along with his commentaries. In this way Lü took advantage of the very system he repudiated in order to reach an audience whose political ambitions and utilitarian motives would lead them to study him. There, embedded in his commentaries on the Four Books (*Great Learning, Mean,* the *Analects,* and *Mencius*), one finds his radical political views.

Like many of his Sung predecessors, Lü was a "restorationist" who tended to reject existing dynastic institutions as flawed and corrupt in comparison to those of high antiquity. Hence not only was his stance far from conservative of the status quo, it was no less than radical in its attack on the established order. Late Sung reformers, and even Chu Hsi in his more seasoned judgments, found it necessary to moderate that critique and make concessions to the fact of historical change, so as to come to terms with existing realities. When Lü in the late seventeenth century reaffirms the earlier Sung view, it thus involves still more: the repudiation of another five centuries of dynastic rule, which in turn implies a far more intransigent defense of the original Neo-Confucian position, as well as a refusal to accept any responsibility on the part of Neo-Confucianism for the unhappy outcome in the Ming.

This position rests for Lü, as it did not for early Sung reformers, on the more fully developed Neo-Confucian doctrine of human nature. Here Heaven's Imperative (*t'ien-ming,* politically the Mandate of Heaven) is conceived primarily in terms of man's moral nature, the Heavenly principle within. It is the moral imperative inherent in every human mind-and-heart (the "mind of the Way" referred to above) that must be answered to for the validation of any regime's claimed legitimacy. There can be no mandate from Heaven for any ruler or regime that violates the basic life-giving principles constitutive of human nature. Indeed government exists only to advance and enhance those human values, and not to serve the interests of the ruler or ruling house. Lü says:

> During the Three Dynasties every measure the sage-kings took to provide for the people's livelihood and maintain the social order, including the enfeoffment, military, and penal systems, no matter how minute in detail or long-range their consequences, were only instituted for the sake of all-under-Heaven and their posterity . . . Not a thing was done nor was any law enacted simply for the ruler's own enrichment or aggrandizement, nor was the aim [of the ancients] in the slightest to secure for their descendants an estate to be held on to forever, for fear of others trying to seize it. Thus in the *Mean* (*Chung-yung*) was the sages' humaneness acclaimed for the warmth of its earnest solicitude [for the people].
>
> After the Ch'in and Han [however], even though among the many systems and institutions adopted from time to time there may have been some good ones ostensibly of benefit to the people or enriching the world, the underlying motive in government has been purely selfish and expedient, the fear being that otherwise one might suffer the loss of what belonged to one's family . . . This is why Master Chu [Hsi] said that for over two thousand years the way had not been practiced for even a single day.[4]

Elsewhere Lü identifies rulership with Heaven in order to emphasize both the overarching responsibility of the ruler to the people and the universality of the principles that should govern the ruler's conduct: "The Son of Heaven occupies Heaven's Position (*t'ien-wei*) in order to bring together the common human family within the Four Seas, not just to serve the self-interest of one family."[5] Lü explains that during the Three Dynasties the throne was passed on to others with the idea of sharing responsibility, of doing what was best for the people. "Heaven's Imperative in the minds-and-hearts of the people weighed heavily on them, and the world lightly. [Such being the case, as Mencius said,] the sages would not commit even one unrighteous deed or kill even one person, though to do so might gain them the whole world."[6]

Yet after the Three Dynasties this attitude of shared concern disappeared: "Since the Three Dynasties men's mores have changed, so that it has become a utilitarian world. Both one's own [the ruler's own] and the peoples' hearts have lost their correctness. All rites and music, civil and penal administration, institutions and letters [supposedly incorporated in the Rites], as well as the management of resources and men, are governed purely by selfishness."[7] Although some people talk about the ruler's loving and caring for the people, at best under dynastic rule one could not hope for more than was accomplished by Han Kao-tsu and T'ang T'ai-tsung, founding fathers of their respective dynasties, and this, says Lü, fell far short of the peace and order which prevailed under the Three Dynasties.[8]

This line of argument is, of course, quite similar to that of scholars in the Northern Sung who rejected the Han and T'ang as models for their own rulers. Familiar too is the example of the Ch'eng brothers and Chu Hsi, cited by Lü for their trenchant criticism of the rulers of their time, insisting that the latter "rectify their minds-and-hearts and make their intentions sincere."[9] Yet, for all these Sung precedents, there are significant differences of emphasis in Lü's reformulation of them. His situation differs from theirs not only in virtue of the passage of time, during which generations of Neo-Confucian mentors to the throne have failed to accomplish the needed change in attitude, but also in that Lü has no prospect himself of fulfilling this role—lecturing to the emperor or writing admonitory memorials as Chu Hsi and Chen Te-hsiu had done. In consequence of this, we find him addressing not the reigning emperor but all those in the official ranks who should be sharing in the responsibility of rulership. Remembering, as we do, that Lü's audience consisted largely of candidates for office, it is of some importance that he magnifies the role of the minister, while also including officialdom as a whole in his scathing condemnation of those who have failed to fulfill the responsibility of upholding the True Way.

This reformulation of the problem emerges clearly in Lü's analysis of dynastic rule, for the latter is in his eyes the perversion of a ruler-minister relationship posited as the most serious of all moral relations. Some scholars had justified the dynastic system as a nat-

ural extension of the parent-child relationship, and had tried to promote the idea that the ruler was the loving parent of all the people.
Lü dismissed this as a fraudulent claim and instead equated rulership with ministership. The original basis of rulership did not differ
from that of ministership: the only criterion for holding power
should be individual human merit. "Lineal succession is founded
on the parent-child relationship; the passing on of rulership should
be founded on the ruler-minister relation. The former derives from
the principle of humaneness; the latter from that of rightness. On
this basis these two great principles coexisted [in ancient times] and
were never confused. Thus the Heavenly position [rulership] was
originally conferred on the basis of individual worth." [10]

Elsewhere Lü emphasizes that this basic moral relation is rooted
in the nature received from Heaven:

> People understand that the relation between parent and child is in-
> herent in the moral nature received from Heaven; they do not re-
> alize that the same is true of ruler and minister—that it is a natural
> and not an artificial joining of the two. Heaven gives birth to the
> people and establishes rulers and ministers for them. Rulers and
> ministers are for sustaining the life of the people. The minister
> seeks out a ruler to head the government, and the ruler seeks out
> the minister to share in the governing. Together they represent
> Heaven's presence in the world. Thus the ruler's position is called
> "Heaven's position"; official emoluments are called "Heaven's
> emoluments." Heaven's order and Heaven's justice are not some-
> thing the ruler and minister can take and make their own. Though
> there is a definite difference in the honor done to ruler and minister,
> still it is only a difference of one degree in the relative distance be-
> tween them. [11]

Here Lü emphasizes the organic nature of the social order and of
the moral imperatives governing human relations, while in emphasizing "Heaven's positions" and "Heaven's emoluments" he also
echoes Mencius' distinction between moral worth and social status,
as the basic criterion that should govern the relation between ruler
and minister. Here the distinction has added significance in that Lü
clearly distinguishes the ruler / minister relation from a familial
one, and while reaffirming the ruler's "paternal" responsibility for
the whole human family, insists that this responsibility cannot be

met except through a political order conceived not on the family model but on a more generalized pattern of consensual moral relations, as in the case of friend-and-friend. This is another way of saying that he wanted to free the noble man from subordination to an imperial sage claiming parental authority, rather than fulfilling a true paternal responsibility.

In furtherance of this aim to emancipate the minister, Lü insists that the ruler / minister relation, as he has defined it, takes precedence over all others. Indeed, he says that the moral relation between ruler and minister is the most important of all: "The rightness (i) of the ruler / minister relation is of the first importance in the world (yü chung ti-i shih). It is the greatest of the human moral relations. If one does not keep to this principle, then no matter what one's accomplishments or meritorious deeds, they will count for nothing against the guilt so incurred."[12] While the moral responsibility which attaches to this relation is heavy and inescapable—as fixed and unalterable as the imperatives of Heaven's Mandate—this does not mean that the personal relationship between ruler and minister is similarly fixed and unalterable:

> Ruler and minister come together in agreement on what is right (i). If they can agree on what is right, they can form the relation of ruler / minister; if not, they should part, as is the case in the relation between friends. It is not like father and son, or older and younger brother [that is, a blood relation which cannot be changed]. If they do not agree, there is no need for personal resentment or recrimination. If their commitment is not the same, their Way cannot be carried out, and it is best to part.
>
> Parting is in accordance with the rite of ruler and minister, not a departure from that relation. It was only in later times, with the abandonment of the enfeoffment system and adoption of centralized prefectures and counties, that the world came under the control of one ruler and consequently there was "advancement and retirement" [from office] but no parting. When the Ch'in abandoned the Way, they established the "rite" of honoring the ruler and abasing the minister, and created an unbridgeable gap between the one on high and the other below, giving the ruler complete control over the minister's advancement and retirement, while leaving him nowhere to go. That was when the relation of rightness between ruler and minister underwent a complete change.[13]

In consequence of this change the conception of ministership, as well as of rulership, was corrupted when Heaven's authority was no longer recognized:

> After the Three Dynasties, rulers and ministers forgot about Heaven. Rulership came to be thought of as for one's own self-gratification. Ministers thought that life and death, reward and punishment, were all at the ruler's disposal and it could not be otherwise. Thereupon the ruler became honored and the minister abased, with the two completely separated. Government, insofar as it now involved a sharing of power and prestige, could not possibly be shared. Thereupon usurpations and assassinations followed; a world of selfishness and expediency was produced. Cut off from Heaven, rulers did not understand that rites came from Heaven, ministers did not realize that loyalty [being true] was rooted in the moral imperative [and political mandate], that it is principle, and the nature is principle.[14]

Lü completes the argument by charging that it was the disastrous error of Wang Yang-ming's "innate knowing" in subverting principle, by assimilating it entirely into the mind, which frustrated the effort to establish principle in the halls of power. Still Wang's fault was only to thwart the needed reformation; others were to blame for the original corruption. If one compares what Lü has to say about this sorry state of things with what Chen Te-hsiu had said about it earlier in his *Extended Meaning of the Great Learning* (*Ta-hsüeh yen-i*) one notices that Lü has reduced the problem to much simpler terms: he has given up the hope of reforming dynastic rulers, and concentrates far more of his attention on evils prevailing among scholar-officials, who by now have been thoroughly infected by the selfishness, acquisitiveness, and expediency characteristic of dynastic rule.

Properly the role of minister or scholar-official was to speak out against existing evils and abuses. Although the *Mean* 27 speaks of the noble man as, by his very silence, commanding respect through the force of his own character, Lü is concerned lest this be misunderstood as sanctioning the toleration of evil. At court, he says, it is a shame and a disgrace for the noble man if the Way is not carried out. "When he stands at court, there is no way he can keep silence. If something is done contrary to the Way, he can only withdraw from participation in it. To keep silence is what base officials and unworthy scholars do."[15] In the Confucian context, there could be no clearer statement of the need for ministers to exercise a prophetic function.

Since the Ch'in and Han, however, scholar-officials have not only kept silence in the face of evil; they have actively cooperated with it, seeking only to gratify the wishes of the ruler. Even when they have paid lip-service to what was right, in conformity with the rites, they have been motivated by one concern only: to cater to the ruler and advance their own ambitions. This, says Lü, is why they are unwilling to advocate fundamental changes and, indeed, go so far as to argue against restoring the institutions of the sage-kings as impractical.[16]

Parenthetically, we may note a similar criticism of corrupt rulers and acquiescent ministers by Ch'iu Chün (1421–1495) in his *Supplement to the Extended Meaning of the Great Learning* (*Ta-hsüeh yen-i pu*), a work certainly known to Lü.

> At the zenith of the Shang great ministers served their rulers according to the Way. If the ruler in sacrificing to spiritual beings was too parsimonious or too extravagant, then the ministers would remonstrate with him and not let him err . . . In later ages, however, rulers have time and again become intimate with sycophants and have followed heterodox practices . . . They waste wealth and harm the people, bringing on calamitous changes and inviting misfortune and disorder . . . But not only has the ruler erred; at times the great ministers who are supposed to remonstrate remain silent, asking no questions and venturing not a word.[17]

In his own time, says Lü, this situation arises not from any lack of natural sympathy on the part of scholars for the people and their needs, but from the fact that the examination and civil service system mass-produce scholars on the wrong model. "Scholars' mind-and-hearts become like block-prints, and just as errors in the text of the block are reproduced in what is printed, they all repeat the same errors."[18]

Many of the points made by Lü concerning the illegitimacy of dynastic rule are similar to those found in Huang Tsung-hsi's *Plan for the Prince* (*Ming-i tai-fang lu*), where Huang challenges the legitimacy of dynastic law and speaks of it as "unlawful law."[19] Lü resists the idea that fundamental institutions should be thought of in terms of law, preferring to stay with the traditional Confucian view of them as rites, and of law as only a last, coercive recourse when the possibility of voluntary cooperation through rites no longer exists. But he makes a like distinction to Huang's when he speaks of existing institutions in Mencian terms as "rites that are not rite" (*fei-li chih li*) and "rightness that is not right" (*fei-i chih i*). Commenting on this passage in *Mencius* 4B:6, Lü asserts an intrinsic link between rites, rightness, and principles. It is an assertion grounded on two basic Neo-Confucian ideas: that rites are the measured expression of Heaven's principles (*t'ien-li chih chieh-wen*) and that principle is one but its particularizations are diverse (*li-i fen-shu*).

Here one sees that Lü uses "rite" to mean a formulation of principle directly in relation to facts and circumstances. It combines the constancy and universality of principle with its differentiated application to all human affairs, while "right" or "rightness" pertains particularly to the appropriateness of an action in time. Both are indispensable to the employment and fulfillment of principle in the mind. Hence Lü speaks of rites as the substance or embodiment (*t'i*) of the Way. They are not mere residual excrescences of some hidden virtue, as Lao Tzu and Chuang Tzu would have it, or momentary and ephemeral traces of an inconceivable Truth, as the Buddhists would see them, but are indeed the very reality of the Way.[20]

A secondary implication is that "rite," as the formal definition and concrete embodiment of principle, covers some of the same ground as our rational, moral, and legal conception of "rights." Rites express the principles of propriety and respect toward others in the broadest sense—for example, the respect to be shown not only other human beings, but also things and affairs in the world at large, including the entire natural order.

Of special significance is the way Lü relates this conception to the human emotions. Lü believed the emotional and instinctual drives in man always to be accompanied by their corresponding innate principles in the mind-and-heart, with emotions providing the energy and principles the direction for human activities. As Lü puts it:

> Rites derive from Heaven [principle], emotions from the mind-and-heart. Rites are always joined to human emotions, but this

must mean to be in accord with the norms of the highest excellence in human emotions, for example, with Heaven. To weigh the emotions, evaluate them, adjust and modulate, correct and check them, is all according to Heaven. Whether to set rites forth clearly, so that emotions attain their proper fulfillment, or [contrarily] for the emotion alone to be relied upon, allowing Heaven's principles to be overruled—that is the essential difference between orthodoxy and heterodoxy.[21]

Here Lü speaks of the emotions as natural powers or virtues (*te*), while the rites are spoken of as giving formal embodiment to the principles which should guide the appetites:

All human hearts are the same in having desires and [their corresponding indwelling] principles. For instance, they are the same in their love of goods and sex. However, they should only get what it is right for them to love. If one speaks only of their being the same in the love of goods and sex [and not in having principles], then human desires can become a source of great disorder in the world. Therefore when Mencius spoke of what makes human hearts the same, he referred to principle, to what is right and proper. Filiality, brotherliness, and commiseration are common principles of what is right and proper; therefore they are called the Way. Extrapolating from these norms one projects the Way, which is the common basis for putting these principles into practice. Therefore what is spoken of as the "Way of the Measuring Square" refers to taking those common principles for measuring human hearts and making them the means of governance which brings peace to the world. Simply to pursue the satisfaction of the physical appetites and let everyone gratify his own desires is the naturalness and laissez-faire of the Taoists or the expedient adaptability of the Buddhists. It is not the Sages' Way of the Measuring Square.[22]

Critics of Neo-Confucianism in Lü's time and after often criticized its concept of principle and its practice of rites as a deadly attack on the human emotions, reflecting the influence on Neo-Confucianism of Buddhism and Taoism with their negative view of human desires. In Lü's case, however, as in Chu Hsi's,[23] the emotions are not seen as intrinsically evil but as natural. Thus the issue for Lü is whether the norms for directing these desires are not also natural, so that one need not regard human desires as inherently selfish and anarchic.

Here two points should be observed. The first is that Lü treats the matter less as a great struggle for the moral will in overcoming the physical appetites than as a question of recognizing the reality of principle in the universe and in the mind of man—that is, of dealing with the philosophical errors of Buddhism and Taoism. The second point is that when Lü does attack selfishness in man it is almost always in the form of the greed and acquisitiveness of those who hold power and influence over others, through the dynastic system. So far as the common man is concerned, Lü is all sympathy for the satisfaction of their basic physical needs. In this, of course, he is following Mencius, who diagnosed the essential problem as the failure of the ruler and his henchmen to identify with the needs and feelings of the common man.

Indeed, if Lü can be accused of being too moralistic in such matters, it would have to be for reducing the whole problem of dynastic rule simply to a question of selfishness on the part of power holders. This simplistic tendency shows itself in a disinclination to deal in a more realistic way with the historical factors that underlie the development of the dynastic system—as for instance others like Huang Tsung-hsi, Ku Yen-wu, and Wang Fu-chih (1619–1692) did in a more realistic way.[24] More often than not, Lü is content to dismiss these as simply considerations of expediency and utilitarianism, and then to turn the analysis in the direction of those philosophical errors—typified by Wang Yang-ming and other ostensible Confucians but covert Buddhists—which allow principle to be taken as whatever circumstances dictate.

If this is not uniformly the case with Lü, it is because he often detects some other moral issue at stake in the discussion of particular institutions, such as the well-field system of equal landholding or the school system. Often enough he simply refers to the ancient rites or institutions in a formulaic way as "the enfeoffment system, the well-fields, the schools, the penal and administrative systems," but occasionally he can be quite acute in singling out fundamental principles at issue in the neglect or abandonment of such institutions. Thus, for him, a principle underlying the well-field system was its provision of the basic means of subsistence for all, and Lü stubbornly held to this egalitarian economic model against those who believed it to be impossible of realization in existing circumstances. Concerning one such argument, Lü had this to say in his *Recorded Conversations:*

> Someone said that schools are not difficult to set up, but the well-field system is far from easy to carry out, in witness whereof is the fact that today there are schools but no well-fields. To this the Master [Lü] replied: 'They do not realize that the schools of today are not the same as the schools of antiquity. The latter were set up only after the well-fields had been instituted [so essential to them were the well-fields as means of support]. For their whole purpose and organization was linked to the well-field system, which is not at all the case with the schools of today. So if it is easy for one [to be established], it is equally easy for both; and if it is difficult, it is equally difficult for both. There is no difference between them in this.'[25]

Such an argument does not, of course, dispose of the practical difficulties, but it does show an awareness on Lü's part that the existing school system is inadequate (something his questioner had not apparently thought of) and that the educational problem could not be solved except on the basis of an improvement in the economic condition of the ordinary man. Since other Neo-Confucians, as we have seen, were not unconscious of the failure to establish a universal school system of the kind Chu Hsi had advocated, it is significant that Lü has not forgotten the point either.

In this emphasis on the fundamental importance of the common people we see not only a reflection of Mencius' emphasis on the people, but a further application of Lü's basic doctrine that all life comes from Heaven, that all human beings are endowed with the moral nature, and that in each individual lies the imperative to act in accordance with the principles inherent in that nature. It is not a "mandate" solely for the ruler.

All of this is consistent with what Chu Hsi sets forth in his commentary on the opening chapter of the *Great Learning,* but the particular emphasis on Heaven's Imperative comes from the *Mean.* This has special meaning for Lü as the basis for his refutation of Wang Yang-ming's view of the mind-and-heart, but that is not all.

Considering that the *Mean* is the most metaphysical of the Four Books, it is significant how much of Lü's commentary on it is devoted to political and social matters, as if especially to ground the social order in the underlying structure of the universe, and at the same time show how principle, in the form of the human moral nature, must find embodiment in the social order. Thus, discussing the opening lines of the *Mean,* he says, "Whenever one speaks of rites, music, law, and government one is speaking about the moral nature which derives from Heaven's Imperative." [26]

Since the universal moral nature is the most fundamental principle of the social order, and rites are the embodiment of the Way governing human affairs, it establishes a certain basic human equality as the touchstone of government. Speaking to the Ch'eng-Chu doctrine of "renewing the people," Lü says: "Both the common people and the Son of Heaven are rooted in the same principle. Speaking of it in terms of rank from the top down, the *Great Learning* says 'from the Son of Heaven down to the common people,' but in terms of principle, in reality, it goes from the common people up to the Son of Heaven. The Son of Heaven's renewing of the people should proceed on the same principle, and conform to the common man's regulation of his own family." [27] Lü's *Recorded Conversations* adds the further note: "This is not only a responsibility which weighs on the ruler. Everyone has his own self [to govern] and therefore there is no one on whom the responsibility does not lie. Just as there are the myriad things and one Supreme Ultimate, so each thing has its own Supreme Norm to follow." [28]

Although the matter is discussed in terms of responsibilities rather than entitlements, it is clear that "each thing's having its own norm to follow" confers on it a certain irreducible autonomy, which governance must take into account and respect. Thus Lü also says:

> There are many gradations from the Son of Heaven down to the common people, and in performing their own proper function each is different, but the differentiation lies in one's lot or function and not in the principle. Therefore it is said, 'Principle is one and its particularizations diverse . . .' No matter how low the commoner is, it is the same underlying principle and not a different case. The commoner may not have the official function of ordering

the state and bringing peace to the world, but inherent in the fulfilling of his self-cultivation is the principle of ordering the state
and bringing peace to the world.[29]

From this one can see that the structure of authority, which in Lü's
mind derives from the imperative of Heaven, is based on the moral
nature as expressed through the minds and hearts of the common
people, and that it works upward from them, not downward from
the Son of Heaven, in a manner parallel to the workings of the economic principle discussed earlier. This is all of one piece with the
interdependent structure of economic welfare and educational opportunity discussed in relation to the school system.

To one way of thinking, Lü's belief in the enduring character of
principle and of the Way represents the quintessence of his "orthodoxy." Without doubt it is the main theme of his attacks on all
forms of heterodoxy, and it underlies his stubborn adherence to
political ideals at odds with later customs, as well as his upholding
of ancient models in favorable contrast to existing institutions.
Here then lies a seeming paradox: that Lü's radical program and
wholesale rejection of the established order rest squarely on his uncompromising insistence on principles at the heart of Ch'eng-Chu
orthodoxy.[30]

Similarly with Lü's view of the social order. Compared to the
Three Dynasties, everything subsequent to it has become flawed
and corrupt, and even reform efforts have proven to be ephemeral.[31]
Yet, though it has not been possible to restore the institutions of the
sage-kings, "it is absolutely essential that scholars preserve these
principles in order to keep alive the hope of restoration."[32] Whether
they succeed or not, however, the Way remains. "Although the Way
of the Sages has not been practiced for at least two thousand five
hundred years, it is still there. This is what is meant by the Way's
not being lost [in *Analects* 29:22]."[33]

From even this brief summary of Lü's views, one can see how
his critique of dynastic rule and his insistence on meeting the legitimate needs of the common people are clearly grounded in the
Neo-Confucian view of principle and of the rites as giving form
and satisfaction to natural human desires. There is no warrant here
for the view that either principles or rites are to be seen as instru-

ments of human exploitation and oppression. Rather, Neo-Confucian teachings provide a solid philosophical ground for the prophetic stance of the Neo-Confucian in protesting the evils of Chinese autocracy. In fact he comes closer than anyone I know of in traditional China, except Huang Tsung-hsi, to asserting the right and responsibility of the common people to participate in the political process, though he does not spell out how this is to be done except through the family.

As a historical postscript to this summary of Lü's critique of dynastic rule, I should like to draw attention to the posthumous "martyrdom" suffered by this Neo-Confucian "prophet":

> About midway through the Yung-cheng reign, in 1728–29, a revolt broke out against the dynasty. Though it was quickly put down, its leader confessed to having been inspired by the antidynastic views of Lü Liu-liang (1629–1683), who had been a champion of the Chu Hsi revival and a major influence on Lu Lung-chi, himself revered as a beacon of strict Chu Hsi orthodoxy in the early Ch'ing. At this juncture the emperor had Lü Liu-liang punished posthumously and with a vindictive thoroughness. His remains were dug up and exposed to desecration, his family survivors punished, his writings proscribed, and numerous favorable references to him in the works of Lu Lung-chi expurgated. The emperor, who favored Ch'an Buddhism, was not so lost in Ch'an meditation that he would lose such an opportunity to do in the orthodox opposition.[34]

5

Fang Tung-shu, a Prophetic Voice in the Early Modern Age

DURING THE EARLY CH'ING PERIOD, thanks to the efforts of Lü Liu-liang and Lü Lung-chi, the Ch'eng-Chu teaching emerged as something more than just an examination orthodoxy; it grew into an active intellectual force both in and out of court. Meanwhile alongside it a new movement developed, the so-called Han Learning, or School of Evidential Research, which rode the same wave of conservative reaction against alleged Ming subjectivism and libertarianism, but also drew from both Ch'eng-Chu and Wang Yangming schools new developments in critical historical and textual scholarship. These enabled the Han Learning increasingly to assert its own independence, at which point, as the new learning came to stand side-by-side with the established educational orthodoxy, an uneasy coexistence ensued. The latter remained well established in education and the examination system, while the influence of the new criticism was exerted mainly in the field of advanced scholarly research. In both of these spheres the developing contest between them cut across official and nonofficial lines.

Intellectually speaking, the influence of the School of Evidential Research had, by the eighteenth century, become so dominant that Liang Ch'i-ch'ao, in his *Intellectual Trends in the Ch'ing Period* (*Ch'ing-tai hsüeh-shu kai-lun*), would later describe this Han Learning, which "carried on empirical research for the sake of empirical research and studied classics for the sake of classics," as "the orthodox school."[1] This may be too simple a characterization of the Evidential Learning, but Liang's reference to it as "the orthodox school" is symptomatic. That there could be such a new intellectual "orthodoxy" coexisting with an older Ch'eng-Chu orthodoxy in education, as if in some symbiotic relationship, tells us that even the mature Confucian tradition was far from simple and fixed but generated contending forces on more than one level at a time.

Yet the Han Learning had long been entrenched in scholarly circles, as well as among their patrons in high Ch'ing officialdom, when in the early nineteenth century, toward the end of the Ch'ing period, a powerful challenge came from the rear guard of Ch'eng-Chu orthodoxy in the writings of Fang Tung-shu (1772–1851). A sharp controversialist himself, Fang has also been seen as a highly controversial figure by intellectual historians, and recognized as perhaps the most articulate spokesman for the Ch'eng-Chu school in his time. Liang Ch'i-ch'ao said of Fang's treatise *Reckoning with the Han Learning* (*Han-hsüeh shang-tui*), written in 1824, that "its courage in opposing [the "orthodox" school] made it a kind of revolutionary work."[2] Other modern writers like Hu Shih, by contrast, have seen Fang as leading a last reactionary outburst against the Han Learning on behalf of the decadent remnants of Neo-Confucianism, defending their sacred textual ground against the higher criticism.[3] Fang came from a family of scholars identified with the T'ung-ch'eng school, which had attempted to revive the prose style and thought of the neoclassical movement in the Sung, represented in literature by Ou-yang Hsiu (1007–1072) and in philosophy by Chu Hsi. Fang had little success in rising through the examination system, and spent most of his life as an impecunious tutor in private homes, lecturer in local academies, or scholarly aide to high officials. If this suggests an insecure, marginal existence on the edge of the literocratic elite, such a dependent condition, economically speaking, in no way inhibited Fang's independence as a scholar and thinker. His outspoken views commanded attention, if not always assent. Fearless in challenging eminent scholars and high officials alike, he faulted the former for their scholarly errors and philosophical bankruptcy, the latter for the inadequacies of China's foreign policy and national defense.

One of the most frequent targets of Fang's criticism, Juan Yüan (1764–1849), was a highly respected scholar of the Han Learning, a senior official, and governor-general of Kuangtung and Kwangsi, whose policies Fang openly censured even while his livelihood as a scholar depended on Juan's patronage of a major scholarly project in 1821–1822. That Fang could speak so boldly, despite his low status, is an indication of the high regard in which his scholarship and opinions were held. Indeed the breadth and depth of his scholarship were most impressive. Contrary to the view of earlier twentieth-century scholars that the T'ung-ch'eng school was characterized by a "bigotry . . . which limited [the school] to the study of Chu Hsi's commentaries and to the prose-writing of a few men, branding other types of literature as harmful to the mind,"[4] Fang's learning actually stands as testimony to the Chu Hsi school's pursuit of "broad learning." This extended to the in-depth study of all the major schools of Chinese thought, including Buddhism, Taoism and—even more rare—some ventures into Japanese *kangaku* scholarship. While the same might equally be said of an eclectic scholar-dilettante, Fang's seriousness as a scholar is attested to by the notably analytic and penetrating critiques he made of other thinkers and schools.[5]

Fang is best known, however, for his *Reckoning with the Han Learning*,[6] which features a detailed list of charges against scholars of the Evidential Research movement, giving point-by-point rebuttals. Thus we are not surprised to find it often fiercely argumentative and polemical in tone. Like other champions of orthodoxy before him, Fang speaks with the voice of the Neo-Confucian prophet condemning a wayward generation of scholars and officials for their failure to keep to the true Way. No doubt this combative manner reflects the psychological burden borne by anyone who challenges the establishment, whether scholarly or official, as Fang himself seems to have realized.[7] Yet a more careful reading of Fang's work reveals a more complex picture, balancing the prophetic and scholarly roles in the tradition.

Like Lü Liu-liang in the early Ch'ing, Fang has his Neo-Confucian heroes: Chang Lü-hsiang and Lu Lung-chi,[8] proponents of the Ch'eng-Chu school in the early Ch'ing whom he regards as its only authentic transmitters.[9] (By this time the official condemnation of Lü Liu-liang and proscription of his works would have made it difficult for Fang to incur or acknowledge any direct debt to Lü.) Fang, too, has his villains—most of the leading figures in the Han Learning movement from Ku Yen-wu on down. The Han Learning is thus Fang's bête noire, as the Wang Yang-ming school had been Lü's earlier. Nevertheless there is much significance in their different choices of heroes (or ancestors) to be venerated and in their treatment of the villains who have betrayed the Ch'eng-Chu legacy.

Fang, like Lü, intimates that he feels it incumbent on himself to take up the prophetic mantle last worn by Chang and Lu,[10] but he is not so dismissive of other Neo-Confucians and is much less inclined than Lü Liu-liang to write off long centuries of history as mere wasteland stretching between the early prophets Confucius and Mencius and the later Ch'eng brothers and Chu Hsi. This may be seen in part from his handling of the Han Learning itself. What Fang excoriates in this latter-day movement is its misappropriation of Han dynasty scholarship for its own dubious purposes. On the whole he sees Han dynasty scholars like Tung Chung-shu, Yang Hsiung, and Cheng Hsüan as having rendered an important service to the preservation of the Confucian tradition. After the repressions of the Ch'in dynasty and burning of the books, it was an indispensable contribution of these early scholars to have preserved the classic texts, even in fragmentary and confused form, so as to pass them on to later generations.[11] And even though the T'ang commentators, like K'ung Ying-ta, could do no more than simply conserve and codify the surviving texts, they too performed a necessary task of preservation and transmission.[12]

For all this, however, the Han and T'ang dynasties were far from propitious ages for the reestablishment of sagely rule or the repossession of the sages' teaching. This left to the Sung the task of philosophical reconstruction, which the Ch'engs and Chu did brilliantly, grasping the "whole substance and great functioning" of the Way by "following the texts and discerning the mind of the sages."[13] Yet, successful though this effort was in producing a long line of scholars devoted to broad learning and critical study of the classics (contrary to *Han hsüeh* assertions),[14] the synthesis achieved by the Ch'eng brothers and Chu Hsi could not but suffer at the hands of idiosyncratic interpreters.[15] Lu Hsiang-shan diverged from it, Wang Yang-ming distorted it, and finally the latter-day school of Evidential Research which claimed to speak for Han Learning virtually discarded Sung philosophy in favor of philological studies—mere displays of technical virtuosity and recondite antiquarianism that distracted scholars' attention from the central human concerns of the Confucian tradition. Thus the so-called Han Learning of the Ch'ing did not measure up to the responsibility bequeathed to it. Scholars of the Evidential Learning failed to preserve and uphold the legacy of the Sung even to the extent that Han scholars had conserved the Confucian learning of the Chou dynasty.[16] Instead they openly repudiated Sung learning. Hence their claim to fulfill the mission of Han Learning was itself false, and having defaulted on this basic obligation to carry on the succession, they could stake no claim to speak for the tradition as a whole.

From this rough account, one gets Fang's sense of the continuity and cumulative character of the tradition, so much in contrast to the prophetic version which had downplayed and downgraded Han and T'ang scholarship in order to highlight the extraordinary insights of the Sung masters into the true depths of the sages' mind. From his discussion of the matter elsewhere, we know that Fang was highly conscious of the problem of continuity/discontinuity in the Succession to the Way, and even compared the post–Chu Hsi era to the long lapse in effective articulation of the Way after Mencius.[17] As both scholar and prophet himself, he can invoke either side of the tradition depending on the nature of the occasion or the purpose to be served. Thus in a long essay on the nature of the Way, in a collection of his prose writings wherein Fang takes the offensive against Buddhism and the Han Learning, he dwells on their deceptive and misleading character, while glorifying the heroic role of such figures as Mencius, Han Yü, Ou-yang Hsiu, the Ch'eng brothers, and Chu Hsi.[18]

In one of his prefaces Fang offers an almost classic definition of the Confucian sage as prophet: "'The great source of the Way is Heaven.' Heaven does not speak, but it gives birth to the sages, who speak for it. The words of the sages are all for explicating the Way in order to awaken the world and proclaim its principles."[19] Thus the words of the sages are like signs from Heaven. There is here no such claim as we find in the Old Testament and the Quran that God himself speaks directly to man through the prophet (the credibility of which puts an extra demand on the faith of the hearer), but in the Confucian case, though "Heaven does not speak," the sages nonetheless speak for it. The setting may be more humanistic (as compared to the more theistic character and I-Thou relationship of the Semitic religions), but the moral burden falls, if anything, still more heavily on the Confucian noble man, who alone can break through the prevailing cant and convention to give clear voice to the true Way.

If in this fashion the tension is sustained between the high moral standard identified with Heaven and the corrupt state of the world as adjudged by the Confucian noble man, in other places Fang just as clearly sustains the claims of the received tradition. It is one that has, even in the most decadent times, produced heroic protest. Thus, in many prefaces Fang celebrates the collective achievement of scholars in the late Ming, whose philosophical views he might sometimes question but whose sacrifice of their lives in resisting corruption and oppression kept the flame of the Way continuously burning.[20]

A major theme of the *Reckoning* is the continuing debate over the Han Learning's primary concern with evidential research in historical linguistics and text criticism, on the one hand, and the primacy of moral principles among orthodox Neo-Confucians, on the other.[21] Fang's objection to the former is on grounds of priority, not principle. Philology and phonology have for him a genuine instrumental value but, however sophisticated in technique, still no more than that. They are among the language skills which, according to the classical definition, had been classed as "elementary learning" (*hsiao-hsüeh*) preparatory to the higher studies discussed in the *Great Learning*. Indeed by Fang's time *hsiao-hsüeh* had come to have the secondary meaning of "philology." Yet from his point of view the top priority given to philology by the Han Learning has stood things on their head. Scholarly specialization has taken to solving philological puzzles and antiquarian conundrums rather than to dealing with the larger human issues of self-cultivation, order in the family, disorder in the state, and peace in the world—all involving moral principles and thus, for Fang, the moral mind.[22] Fang pays special tribute to his forebear Fang Pao (1668–1749), an early leader of the T'ung-ch'eng school, who had evoked the reformist spirit of the Northern Sung scholars with their primary concern for the larger meaning (*ta-i*) or general sense of the classics.[23] In this there is a notable resemblance also to Lü Liu-liang.

Fang too has his own prophetic warning and message to convey. This involves an aspect of his thought much discussed in the final chapter of his *Reckoning,* but rarely noted if at all by modern writers: the importance to him of human discourse and open discussion (*chiang-hsüeh*) as means of advancing the Way. *Chiang-hsüeh* has often been translated as "lecturing," and it may be that in later times *chiang-hsüeh* had become so routine as to approximate mere lecturing. But there is another term *chiang-i* (*kōgi* in Japanese) more often used for formal lectures in both Chu Hsi's time and Fang's, and Chu himself made some distinction between the two. As it was understood among Neo-Confucians and by early historians of Neo-Confucianism, *chiang-hsüeh* ("discursive learning") had the clear implication of dialogue, group discussion, and even something approximating our "public discussion."[24] "Public" might be misleading if it conjured up a picture of modern publicists at work, a substantial Fourth Estate, or the availability of media for wide communication that would contribute to the formation of "public opinion" in the current idiom. Such agencies did not exist in Sung and Ming China. The implicit original context is one of discussion among scholars, or in any case among a comparatively limited, literate social stratum, as well as one of debates largely carried on in schools and academies.

The high-water mark for this kind of discussion came in the mid and late Ming, when Wang Yang-ming's liberal, and in some branches of his "school" populist, version of Neo-Confucianism stimulated political discussion and popular education even among the illiterate or quasi-literate segments of society. After the Ch'ing conquest many writers, across a broad spectrum of philosophical allegiances, attributed the fall of the Ming to the divisiveness aroused in the sixteenth century by this kind of open discussion, free thinking, and partisan controversy. Ku Yen-wu was only the most prominent of the writers who considered the Ming to have been divided and weakened for foreign conquest by such controversy.

As Fang lays out his rebuttal, he challenges first the assertion that the Sung learning had neglected serious study of the classics in favor of free speculation. He offers a string of quotations from Chu Hsi in which the latter had urged students not to neglect the Han and T'ang commentarial literature on the classics, while at the same time he had regretted that Han and T'ang scholars, preoccupied with philological and exegetical matters, had lost sight of the "larger meaning" (ta-i) of the classics, including both the ultimate questions of the Way, virtue, nature, and destiny, and the major proximate questions of self-cultivation and the urgent needs of human society.[25] Such being the case, anyone seriously committed to "Learning for One's Self" was left to conclude that, inasmuch as Han and T'ang scholars offered no rational answers to such questions, one could only resort to intuitive means, introspecting the mind while neglecting things outside or beyond oneself. This, Fang says, was truly to "fall into the emptiness of Buddhism and Taoism."[26]

Fang goes on to address the further charge that open discussion encourages partisanship and sectarianism, which do violence to the family and state. This he categorically rejects; on such grounds one could repress virtually all criticism and dissent. In Fang's view anyone who expressed alarm over dangers to state and society could expect to be labeled a partisan (tang), or a follower of the "Learning of the Way" (tao-hsüeh), or "an adherent of the discussion of learning" (chiang-hsüeh men-hu).[27] Critics of the Sung school have alleged that it was the partisan divisions between the Loyang and Ssuch'uan schools that sowed the seeds of the Northern Sung's destruction, while they place none of the blame where it belongs—on Ts'ai Ching, supposedly the responsible head of government at that time. Similar accusations have been made concerning the School of the Way (tao-hsüeh) and the fall of the Southern Sung, without mentioning the repressive role of Han T'o-chou, then prime minister, in proscribing that school. Finally, the fall of the Ming is all blamed on the partisanship of the Tung-lin group, who were out of power, while such powerful personages as Yen Sung and the eunuch Wei Chung-hsien are held in no way responsible.[28]

How can one fault the Confucians for what has happened when their advice has gone unheeded? Who can blame Confucius for the weakness of the state of Lu, or Mencius for the disorders of the Warring States Period? Similarly with the fall of the Ming: How can this be attributed to the partisan spirit engendered by the Tung-lin's open advocacy of Neo-Confucian principles? Rather, it was to the credit of the Tung-lin leaders that, being concerned lest the larger meaning and basic principles of the classics be lost, they assembled scholars to discuss them. This was necessary because scholars at court, even those in high office, dared not speak out against the evils of the day.[29]

Here Fang's views are no doubt colored by the sense of powerlessness that attaches to his nonofficial status on the margin of the literocratic elite. Whether or not one identifies him, in that condition, as an independent scholar (one free of the responsibility that goes with holding office), or as one still dependent for his marginal existence on the patronage of officials, Fang chose to identify himself with those literati who felt a Confucian obligation to speak out. Whatever the limiting circumstances, he assumed the special role and burden of the prophet—the warner and protester against a soft and self-indulgent generation.

For Fang, many of the most celebrated teachings of the classics could be called "the discussion of learning," including the moral instructions in the *Book of Documents* and *Rites of Chou;* Confucius' teachings in answer to questions about humaneness (*jen*), government, the noble man, etcetera in the *Analects;* Mencius' "Learning extensively and discussing minutely" (IVB, 15); the *Great Learning*'s steps of rectifying the mind, making the intention sincere, regulating the family, and so on—any of these matters "from the self to the state and nation, from a single item to the myriad kinds of affairs, what is there not subject to discussion?" Therefore Confucius said (in the *Analects* 3:7), "Not to discuss thoroughly what is learned . . . is something I would be concerned about."[30]

Those responsible for maintaining the water courses, says Fang, will spare no effort to keep them open to traffic and communication. But compared to the blocking of water courses, the shutting of the mouths of the people is far worse. Here Fang evokes an incident reported in the opening chapter of the classic *Discourses of the States* (*Kuo-yü*) purportedly representing the protest of the Duke of Shao against the tyrannical rule of King Li of the Chou dynasty. The latter had suppressed all those who dared to criticize him, and was pleased with the apparent success of his repression. But the Duke of Shao said: "You have merely dammed them up. But stopping up the mouths of the people is more dangerous than stopping up a river. When a river is blocked and then breaks through, many persons are bound to be injured, and it is the same with the people. Therefore one who desires to control a river will leave an opening where the water can be drawn off. And one who would control the people should do likewise, encouraging them to speak." [31]

When Confucius discussed the steps for achieving personal integrity, he spoke first of extensive study, judicious inquiry, careful reflection, and discriminating judgment, and only after that of following these up with earnest practice of the course of action so considered. "Hence," says Fang, "if learning is not discussed, the Way will not be made clear, and if the Way is not made clear, how can one be sure of properly carrying it out in one's personal conduct?" [32] (*Mean* 19).

In the transmission of the Way, only when one discusses it can others hear about it, receive it, and carry it on. Accordingly Mencius talks about the way in which those who first learn of the Way apprise and arouse to action those who come after (5A:7). The *Book of Changes* speaks of the noble man discussing with his friends the practice of virtue (Hexagram 58), while the opening passage of the *Analects*[33] speaks of practicing what one has learned in the company of friends who have come from afar, and of "making friends through letters and enhancing one's humanity [through such intercourse] with friends" [12:24].[34]

From these passages emphasizing the need for discussion of one's practice of virtue in the company of others, Fang goes on to a lengthy recital of other classical examples of the ruler consulting with his ministers in the making of decisions and fostering discussion among the people in order to ascertain their views on correct policies. Numerous cases in history are also cited of the beneficial results of such consultation with the people and the unfortunate consequences of rulers or their ministers failing so to consult. Moreover Fang also notes that Chu Hsi in formulating his Articles of the White Deer Grotto Academy specifically charges its students with the need to discuss the guiding principles of the school as a basis for their voluntary observance of its stated aims—much to be preferred over the imposition of any coercive or punitive regulations.[35]

From the foregoing much-abbreviated synopsis of Fang's argument, one may perhaps glimpse some of the importance Fang attaches not just to debating the issues raised by the Han Learning itself, but to arguing the need for scholarly debate on fundamental issues other than the purely scholarly, and above all for open discussion of questions involving the Confucians' traditional concern for "world-ordering" as an ever-present responsibility. These are matters he could easily have avoided had his motive been only the defense of scholarly turf. Instead, impelled by a sense that the very heart of the tradition was at stake, he went to extraordinary lengths to establish the ground in tradition from which he spoke—the classical examples of Confucius and Mencius engaged in dialogue and debate; the Sung revival of this Confucian advocacy and activism, along with its deeper philosophical probing of the principles which differentiate this reformism from Buddhism and Taoism; and later the heroic efforts of the Tung-lin movement to reassert this activism.

Especially significant in the Ch'ing context, and against the background of the Ch'ing scholarly establishment, is Fang's insistence on the role of schools and academies as centers of discussion and debate. Earlier Huang Tsung-hsi, in his *Plan for the Prince* (*Ming-i tai-fang lu*), had made the same point, only to have it largely ignored through the long Ch'ing dominance—and also, we may be reminded, the dominance of the Ch'ing scholarly "orthodoxy" which Liang Ch'i-ch'ao had identified with the school of Evidential Research.

Fang, however, had his own experience of this kind of academic research as a scholar attached to major scholarly projects at leading academies in the Canton area, including the Hsüeh-hai t'ang Academy, center for the production of the monumental compendium of Ch'ing commentaries and treatises on the classics, the *Huang Ch'ing ching-chieh* in 1,400 chüan and 366 volumes, under the patronage and direction of the governor-general Juan Yüan. Whether Fang was aware of it or not, support for this academy and its projects more than likely came in part from profits of the opium trade and official collusion with it.[36] Nor did Fang need to know this in order to feel keenly, as he did, that the kind of classical scholarship conducted there, though respectable enough in its own way, fell far short of meeting the academies' responsibility for speaking out against an undoubted evil like the opium trade and the threat of encroaching foreign military power.[37] To do this they would have to concern themselves with principles, not just facts. Earlier a frequent complaint of Neo-Confucian reformers against schools and academies was that they put studying for the civil service examinations ahead of genuine "Learning for One's Self." Now a new scholarly disinterestedness had proven an even greater threat to such genuine learning and cultivation.[38]

Thus Fang's extraordinary emphasis on Confucian moral advocacy had immediate contemporary relevance as well as significance for the revival of tradition. Present dangers required decisive action, not more study of the past—unless it would be study of the kind that had inspired reformers in the Sung and late Ming. Needed now was the large vision of a Chu Hsi combined with definite courses of action in keeping with basic human principles—in effect, Chu's teaching of the "whole substance and great functioning." What was missing, and most urgently required in the present situation, was a new attitude of mind capturing the old message of the mind as Chu Hsi had formulated it.[39] Hence his extended discussion of that message as (1) the "transmission of the mind," contra Ku Yen-wu; (2) the measure or norm in the conscientious mind making the necessary value judgments; and (3) the method of the mind, involving discussion and debate so that action can be guided by the collective judgment and experience of educated men.

Fang's renewed emphasis on the Ch'eng-Chu philosophy of mind and human nature, as well as the practical application of this to the conduct of contemporary affairs, arises from his sense of the moral bankruptcy of the Han Learning, shown in the inability of the value-free, facts-for-facts sake approach of the reigning scholarship to meet the demands of the Confucian social conscience in responding to current crises.

As a remedy Fang reaches back to the Ch'eng-Chu sixteen-word formula concerning the human mind and mind of the Way, believing it to represent the essential thinking of Confucius and Mencius, rearticulated in new terms by Ch'eng-Chu in order to counter the Ch'an view of the mind. For Fang this message and method remain the very heart of the Confucian/Ch'eng-Chu teaching. Though he does not (except when refuting Ku Yen-wu)

refer to it often as either *hsin-fa* or *hsin-hsüeh,* the distinction between the human mind and mind of the Way is central to all of his
discussions, not only in this best known of Fang's tracts, *Reckoning
with the Han Learning,* but in numerous essays in his collected writings dealing with the Way, Heaven, Human Nature, Principle, Qui-
escence, and so forth.[40]

This formula Fang connects with Chu Hsi's interpretation of
the "investigation of things and extension of knowledge" (including his conception of a cumulative learning process leading to a
"breakthrough to integral comprehension")—thus blending the
moral and affective with the rational and cognitive aspects of the
mind. For him this is the true Learning of the Mind-and-Heart,
echoing what Chu Hsi himself had originally said about the message of the mind. Nothing had been forgotten.

Fang's view of the Way is cumulative and collective, not in the
evolutionary or progressive sense, but in recognizing the contributions of many scholars at different stages of history. He sees it not
as a static tradition but a growing one, for which his preferred analogy is typically organic and agrarian: the successive efforts of sow-
ers, cultivators, and reapers in the growing of grain.[41] In the process, there is some loss caused by the errors and failings of those
who stray from the Way, but this may be balanced by the heroic
achievements of scholars like the Ch'eng's and especially Chu Hsi.

Another way of putting this is to say that Fang, though orthodox in balancing the prophetic and scholastic view of the tradition,
avoided a narrow fundamentalism. The assumption of the Evidential Research scholars was that one could get at the original, literal
meaning of the classics, and peel away all subsequent accretions to
get at the pure teaching of the ancients. Fang reminded them that
there were important truths in the *Analects* not found in the earlier
classics, and further advances made by Chu Hsi in meeting the
challenge of Buddhism, which had been unknown in Confucius'
time. Simply returning to the original source was not enough.

6

The Prophet
and the People

GIVEN THIS STATE OF AFFAIRS in the mid-nineteenth century, what can we say, in sum, about "the trouble with Confucianism" or the prophetic voice of the Confucian noble man as it encountered the modern West? Let us consider the question at the point where Fang Tung-shu leaves it in the concluding pages of his *Reckoning with the Han Learning*—with the importance of promoting the active discussion of public issues.

If, as Fang claims, the sage-kings, Confucius, Mencius, and all the great Confucians had urged the indispensability to the political process of open discussion or "learning by discussion" (*chiang-hsüeh*); if, moreover, it had already been a distinguishing mark of the Confucians, according to Li Ssu in the third century B.C., that they "talked together about the Odes and Documents" as a way of invoking the past to criticize the present; and if, after the rise of the learning of the Way (*tao-hsüeh*) as an outgrowth of *chiang-hsüeh* in the Sung,[1] generations of Neo-Confucians, following the Ch'eng brothers and Chu Hsi, had insisted on scholarly criticism and the open airing of political means and ends—then how is it that, in Fang's own estimation, so little had come of this by the late Ch'ing period? If indeed Fang himself represents a still vital, self-critical Confucian tradition, one naturally asks why its capacity for self-renewal did not operate to greater effect, or show more transformative power, in enabling China to meet the challenges of the nineteenth and twentieth centuries?

A full answer to such questions lies beyond the reach of this book, but having ventured earlier to *compare* examples of Confucian protest to the prophets of the West, I should like at this juncture to refer again to my earlier contrast between China and the West on the question of how the prophet relates to "*the* people" as distinct from "*a* people." This applies also to how we understand "public" service, whether in the sense of meeting a common need or shared interest, or of serving "a public," understood as a body of people actively engaged or effectively represented in public affairs. The question here is whether transformative power can be understood solely in relation to the ideas and ideals propounded by prophets and carried forward by traditional elites, or as a tension between the transcendent and the mundane, without also considering how "prophets" have related historically to "a people" or "a public."

If I speak of this more particularly with respect to the "troubles" Confucianism got itself into, I reiterate that this implies no general judgment of a kind so easily and widely reached, both in East and West, concerning the "modern failure" of either China or Confucianism. My intention is simply to address the critical questions Confucians have asked themselves, or would acknowledge as fair and relevant in view of their own avowed aims and historical projects.

The central question, I would say, pertains to the Confucians' roles as officials, scholars, and teachers. While Confucius had said that learning should be for the sake of one's own self-understanding and self-development, rather than to win the approval of others or acquire political success, it was still the social dimension of this self and its engagement in public life that most distinguished Confucius' conception of self as he set it forth to the gentlemen of his time. From the beginning, Confucians had accepted a responsibility for counselling rulers and training men for social and political leadership, as expressed in the ideal of the noble man. From the start too they considered learning and scholarship to be indispensable to the performance of these functions.

It is no less true that their view of learning underwent change over time, as the Confucians responded to new challenges. Expansive periods of intellectual and philosophical growth alternated with phases of retrenchment in which fundamentalist instincts demanded a regrounding of the tradition, as if to keep scholarly inquiry from straying too far from its moral and social base, or, at the opposite extreme, moral zeal from blinding itself to facts. Thus the greatest Confucian minds have managed something of a balance between loyalty to core values and the continued pursuit of "broad learning" through scholarly investigation. Nathan Sivin has reminded me that the intensely orthodox Lü Liu-liang had a strong interest in Western science and contributed significantly to medical learning. Likewise Fang Tung-shu, while complaining of a philology pursued at the expense of moral philosophy, accepted philology and text criticism themselves as necessary branches of learning and on his own part engaged in "the pursuit of truth through facts."

One can of course ask whether this pursuit of truth, as conceived in Confucian humanistic terms, would ever lead to the kinds of speculation being advanced in the West during the eighteenth and nineteenth centuries. Jerome Grieder, in his review of Benjamin Elman's *From Philosophy to Philology,* asked why Ch'ing evidential scholarship, though methodologically innovative, remained "epistemologically sterile." "'Why no Newton in China?'" he says, "has become almost a dismissive cliché. Should we not be asking instead (or as well) 'Why no Kant?'"[2]

That kind of question, if fairly and fully explored, would lead us off into the kinds of trouble the West got into, whereas it is enough here to deal with the troubles Confucians faced—questions such as Fang Tung-shu left us with at the end of his *Reckoning with the Han Learning:* the failure to sustain the kind of discussion and consultation he considered vital to the promotion of the common welfare.

In the early and mid-twentieth century this question went unaddressed by most modern scholars, no doubt on the widespread but mistaken assumption that the fault lay with the Confucians for their alleged elitism—their unwillingness to share literacy and learning with the masses, and their alleged tendency to reserve education to the upper classes. This, the prevalent theory went, prevented the great majority of Chinese from any significant participation in public affairs. There is some truth in this idea but it fails to credit the actual intention of the Confucians to do quite otherwise—to share learning as widely as possible with the people.

The leading Confucian reformers of the Northern Sung period (eleventh and early twelfth centuries) had been advocates of universal schooling. Chu Hsi in the late twelfth century had picked up the same issue and underscored it in the preface to his commentaries on the *Great Learning,* making a special point of the need for schools in every town and village and not just for education in the home or private academy. Neo-Confucian statesmen advanced such a program at the court of Khubilai in the thirteenth century. Others at the founding of the Ming did the same, and at the end of Ming, writers like Huang Tsung-hsi and Lü Liu-liang in the late seventeenth century (to mention only two outstanding cases) took up the same cause. Yet, despite this recurrent advocacy, and despite even actual decisions from time to time to implement such programs by imperial decree, little had come of them. Even in the schools that did get built, as Chang Po-hsing, champion of Chu Hsi orthodoxy in the high Ch'ing, complained, education was too much oriented to the civil service examination, and failed to achieve Chu Hsi's liberal, humanistic aim that education should advance the moral renewal and cultural uplift of the people as a whole, serving broader, more fundamental, purposes than simply bureaucratic recruitment.[3] *but ycause the orig.end of exams was to everone broad culture in buream*

One could explain this failure in part by pointing to certain basic facts of life in China. As an agrarian society, with a dense population depending upon intensive agriculture, China and its farming families felt strong economic pressures to keep the young and able-bodied laboring in the fields rather than release them for work in the study or school. Throughout the land, even the poorest peasants may have prayed for their offspring to be so well endowed with scholarly talents that they might succeed in the examinations, but as a practical matter few would be able to fulfill such an ambition. Moreover, the imperial bureaucracy, though dominating most areas of national life, was not sizable enough and possessed of enough offices to absorb large numbers of candidates, however eager and promising they might appear to be. Lacking too was any substantial middle class that could provide alternative careers or could support, with their surplus wealth and leisure, cultural pursuits or institutions substantially independent of the literocracy and the official establishment (or at least not sufficiently so as to constitute attractive, alternative paths of educational advancement).

Similarly with respect to what in the West would be called the "church." Religious organizations in China were fragmented, with little of either horizontal or vertical structures. They offered no broad institutional base for schools, colleges, or universities such as the church supported in the West. Religious vocations there were, but these led in radically different directions from secular education. Training for the religious life was commonly understood to demand disengagement from established society and culture, if not to pursue monastic disciplines then at least to master esoteric rituals that would relieve people's sufferings and bring surcease from the bitter struggle of life.

What might seem to pass as a "church," in the form of a religious hierarchy beyond the local level, was most often simply a loose family relationship. Temples were identified customarily by forms of religious praxis, rather than by schools of doctrine. Superintendents of religious bodies were appointed by the throne, not elected or chosen by any independent constituency. Instead of springing up organically from some autonomous grass-roots community or representing a creedal congregation, they served at best as intermediaries between the ruler and his people. In many cases indeed they functioned simply as extensions of central authority, though often that authority emanated from the inner palace and was linked to the imperial family rather than to the civil administration.

The resulting pattern, then, was marked by ironies and paradox, with a dominant Confucian tradition that exalted learning and insisted on its wide diffusion as the sine qua non of a viable political and social order, yet found itself incapable of realizing its educational aims except on the basic level of the family or in the higher but much more restricted sphere of the ruling elite. In contrast to this stood a welter of clan cults and native or hybrid popular faiths, answering to the religious needs of the common people but participating hardly at all in government, secular learning, or practical education. Thus, among the peasant masses religion remained as out of touch with higher learning and with rational discourse on public issues as the Confucians were removed from the dynamics of religious faith in the "hearts and minds of the people."

In *East Asian Civilizations* I pointed to the growing realization on the part of late-nineteenth-century reformers like K'ang Yu-wei and Liang Ch'i-ch'ao that the failure in education had been a crucial factor in China's inability to mobilize its human resources against the challenge of the West and Japan. Some of these same reformers, as well as even conservative critics of reform, agreed that the obvious lack of a unified national consciousness betrayed a failure of leadership to reach the "hearts and minds" of the people. Some contrasted this perceived weakness of China to the unifying power of nationalism in Japan and the West, and some saw the power of the latter to mobilize peoples' energies as further linked to the religious dynamism of Shinto and Christianity—whence K'ang Yu-wei's belated and futile attempt in the early twentieth century to recast Confucianism as a state religion, in the erroneous belief (of a kind to which mandarins, both traditional and modern, have been so prone) that a state religion could serve the purpose just as well as a popular faith or mass religious movement.

It is perhaps significant too that many of these reformers, in both nineteenth-century Japan and China, saw their own crisis as prefigured, philosophically speaking, by the split in Neo-Confucian ranks between Wang Yang-ming and the Chu Hsi school, with Wang's emphasis on the moral and spiritual springs of human action standing in contrast to the careful balance Chu Hsi had maintained between the moral and rational, affective and intellective, faculties. One could perhaps argue that such a reconciliation was not inherently implausible or unworkable, as witness the successful blending of Confucian scholarship, feudal loyalties, and Shinto religious beliefs in later Tokugawa and early Meiji Japan. In the conditions of Ch'ing China, however, this fusion was not so easily accomplished. Whether one sees Confucianism as represented by the mandarinate and its civil service mentality, or by the alternative scholarly "orthodoxy" Liang Ch'i-ch'ao identified with the Evidential Research (k'ao-cheng) movement in classical studies, in either case it had proven difficult for Confucians to fulfill all three of the functions their own legacy demanded of them: education for the masses as well as government service and a high level of classical scholarship.

In classical, humanistic learning Ch'ing scholars, arguably, lived up to Chu Hsi's high standards of critical scholarship. Even in terms of human governance, one might allow (notwithstanding the severe negative judgments of a Huang Tsung-hsi, Lü Liu-liang, or Fang Tung-shu) that the Ch'ing record up to 1800 in managing the affairs of so large a country and so massive a population was probably unmatched by any other regime in history. Yet for all this the Confucians fell well short of fulfilling their primitive and perennial vision of achieving Heaven-on-earth through the rule of sage-kings guided by noble men.

This was, of course, a vision of the noble man as prophet, and the failure of the Confucians to achieve it, while no greater than that of any other major world tradition fully to realize its ideals, reminds us again of the original limitations and qualifications of the prophetic office as exercised by the noble man. These had to do with his specific and distinctive commitment to public service (government and education) and humanistic scholarship in ways not typically associated with prophets in the Semitic religions. But it also involved a significant difference between the Confucian concept of Heaven and its Mandate, and the more intensely theistic conception in the Judeo-Christian tradition of a personal god dealing with his human creations both as persons and as a "people."

For the Confucians "the people" were indeed Heaven's creation, and Heaven presided over their fate and fortune in a way expressed by the Mandate of Heaven, with the ruler as the crucial intermediary or surrogate—the "Son of Heaven," who alone offered sacrifice at the Temple of Heaven. As Neo-Confucians like Lü Liu-liang and Fang Tung-shu interpreted this, it was the people who spoke for Heaven and the noble man who spoke to the ruler; but Heaven did not speak directly to its people in the way God spoke through Moses, Isaiah, and Jeremiah to "*His* people," the people with whom He had made a personal contract and covenant. In the language of Jeremiah:

> The days are coming, says the Lord, when I will make a new covenant with the house of Israel and the house of Judah. It will not be like the covenant I made with their fathers the day I took them by the hand to lead them forth from the land of Egypt; for they broke my covenant and I had to show myself their master, says the Lord.

> But this is the covenant I will make with the house of Israel in those
> days, says the Lord. I will place the law within them and write it
> upon their hearts. I will be their God and they shall be my people.
> (Jeremiah 31:31)

In Confucianism, though Heaven's Imperative (or Decree) is, as
the immanent moral nature in all people,[4] likewise "placed within
them and written upon their hearts," the people remain subject to
the ruler, whether to serve him or be the object of his paternal care.
For his part the noble man, in his prophetic role, could be a warner
to the ruler, reminding him of his obligation to provide for the public welfare, but as one committed to public service, as a member of
the ruling class, the noble man ministered to the ruler and, ideally,
as colleague and mentor to the emperor. His function then was to
warn the latter, but apparently not, like Isaiah and Jeremiah, ever to
warn or scold the people, as if they too were active and responsible
participants in the fulfilling of a covenant.

Thus far the discussion has been of the Confucian gentleman or
noble man as minister at court. This is in keeping with the quasi-
prophetic role assigned to the *chün-tzu* as minister in Mencius' discussion of the ruler/minister relation, taking into account that the
text of Mencius is the source for the earliest formulation of ruler/
minister (*chün-ch'en*) as one of the five paradigmatic human relations, and that Mencius is the one par excellence who invested ministership with such a prophetic function.

In the later dynasties, however, after the establishment of centralized bureaucratic administration, the word for "minister," *ch'en,*
could also be understood as referring to any official servant of the
state, even on the lower levels of local government. What then of
the paradigm as it might apply to the local prefect or magistrate?
Or to the Confucian gentleman as a member of the local elite, even
when not holding office but performing nevertheless a leadership
function, if only by virtue of the responsibility which attached to
his status as a person of some education and culture?

In this situation the Confucian gentleman, though not a minister to the people, was at least considered a pastor or shepherd to
them. As an intermediary between the ruler and the people, the
local magistrate was expected to shepherd the people as their guide

and teacher. He also shared in the ruler's responsibility for seeing to the welfare of the people. As intermediary he was charged with reporting to the ruler, through channels, the people's needs. Again, even without formal office, the local elite might perform a role as spokesmen for the people in dealing with the magistrate or prefect. In these connections the people's feelings were certainly to be taken into account, and especially when it was a question of the effect upon the people of governmental actions or the distress caused by natural calamities.

This is not the same thing however, as the local elite's taking on the function of spokesmen for the people in regard to public issues affecting the "state of the nation," so to speak, or the welfare of the people as a whole, beyond the local level. Some individuals of conscience did indeed take it upon themselves to speak out against injustices, or to right wrongs not remedied by official action, as in the case especially of charismatic figures known as "knights-errant" (yü-hsia) so identified because of their bold, chivalrous spirit. But these were striking exceptions, heroic individuals who took the law into their own hands and upheld the cause of "rightness" or "justice" in individual cases. Rarely did they succeed in leading a movement with larger political implications, or if they did it was to found new states or dynasties without significantly altering the basic pattern of ruler / ruled relations.

A more normal and orthodox pattern would be exemplified by the model set by Chu Hsi as prefect. His pastoral care is shown in two forms particularly identified with him: the use of public proclamations (pang) for the edification of the local populace, and the organization of community compacts (hsiang-yüeh). In the former case Chu dealt with a wide range of subjects from matters of public morality to the conduct of agriculture; in the latter Chu tried to provide a mechanism for the promotion of community spirit and a sense of shared responsibility for the community welfare—in effect a meeting place for the discussion of local needs and problems, not for the airing of larger "public" issues. These efforts, at their best, manifested a benevolent paternalism; they give no evidence of a prophetic role or voice on the part of the Confucian gentleman, no matter how conscientious he might be.

For these reasons it is hard to conceive of the Confucian,

whether at court or in the local community, as a "charismatic" leader. Rarely does a Confucian gentleman, even one who may live up to the demanding role of a noble man, exert a magnetic appeal among the people or attract a large personal following that can be turned to political account. Devoted students he may have, admiring scholarly colleagues, and even a local populace appreciative of his administration, but not a political audience or religious following before whom he could perform as a charismatic figure.

What could be at issue here is the sense in which we understand the word "public" in these different contexts, and how this understanding conditions or qualifies the role of the prophet. In classical Confucianism Mencius, the spokesman par excellence for the noble man, underscored the fundamental importance of the "people" (*min*) in politics but the people seen primarily as deserving of leadership responsive to their needs, and only in dire extremity as the people taking action themselves by virtue of the people's natural "right of revolution." Mencius, as we have seen, distinguished between an educated ruling class serving the interests of the "people," and the larger mass of those who worked with their hands and lacked the education and training needed for them to take an active part in government (except when things got bad enough for the people to revolt). In making this distinction Mencius forswore none of his meritocratic, egalitarian principles in favor of a social or political elitism, but only reflected a functional differentiation between leaders and commoners that was already well established by his time (*Mencius* 3A:4). Even the social leveller Mo Tzu affirmed the need for such a functional dichotomy: "[Heaven] desires that among men those who have strength will work for others, those who understand the Way will teach others, and those who possess wealth will share it with others . . . It also desires that those above will diligently carry out their tasks."[5] This state of affairs continued down through the centuries and was not even to be effectively overturned by modern Maoists, with all their commitment to a classless society.

For their part the Neo-Confucians, advocates of universal education in furtherance of the people's welfare but unsuccessful in establishing schools for all, promoted popular education primarily through self-cultivation and disciplined self-governance (*hsiu-chi* chih-jen) in the context of family life and the local community, leaving a considerable gulf between learning on this level and the higher forms of scholarship or of the expertise required in the civil servant. In the absence then of any significant infrastructure between family and local community on the lower level, and the political and cultural organizations of the educated elite on the higher level, there were few channels that could serve as organs of "public opinion" to communicate between the two or support the noble man at court in his service of the public interest.

No doubt this oversimplified model of China's political structure and process will invite challenge from those who can think readily of the infrastructure represented by local and regional organizations of an economic, social, and religious character, which at times played a significant part in Chinese life. The question is, however, whether these were able to perform any role in the political process—that is, address themselves to and carry on a sustained discourse concerning issues of the larger, public interest—to such an extent that either mandarins or scholars would think of the "people" as in any sense an active, corporate body, able effectively to support a sustained political program. More especially it would be a question whether such a program was reformist or radical enough to achieve the transformation of the established order (presumably, in the view of Max Weber and Karl Jaspers, the mission of the prophets).

In the revised version of his *Centrality and Commonality* Tu Weiming emphasizes the continuity between Confucian self-cultivation and the concept of the fiduciary community.

The logic of taking the cultivation of the self and the regulation of the family as "roots" and the ordering of the community, the governance of the state, and universal peace as "branches," may give the impression that complex political processes are reduced to simple relationships explainable in personal familial terms. Yet the dichotomy of root and branch conveys the sense of a dynamic transformation from self to family, to community, to state, and to the world as a whole. Self-cultivation is the root, and harmony attained in the family is a natural outgrowth, like the branch, of our cultivated selves. Family is the root, and harmony attained in the community, the state, and the world is a natural outgrowth of the well-regulated families. In this sense what we do in the privacy of our own homes profoundly shapes the quality of life in the state as a whole.

Nevertheless, it is important to note that the Confucians do not, by stressing the centrality of self-cultivation, undermine the corporate effort that is required for the family, the community, the state, and the world to become humane or fully human. Just as the self must overcome egoism to become authentically human, the family must overcome nepotism to become authentically human. By analogy, the community must overcome parochialism, the state must overcome ethnocentrism, and the world must overcome anthropocentrism to become authentically human. In light of Confucian inclusive humanism, the transformed self individually and corporately transcends egoism, nepotism, parochialism, ethnocentrism, and anthropocentrism to "form one body with Heaven, Earth, and the myriad things."[6]

This I accept as an accurate rendering of the Confucian view of the fiduciary community, inspired by a dynamic conception of the transformative power of self-cultivation, leading outward and upward from self and family through the universal state and even to the universe itself. As rendered by Tu, this process corresponds closely to the continuum in the program of human cultivation and political transformation set forth in the famous eight items or steps of the *Great Learning*. There, however, the word "community" is missing. Notwithstanding this absence, as Tu repeats the series again and again, from self and family to state and world, we notice that he regularly inserts the word "community" in the sequence from family to state. One may well believe (as Tu does, and I myself would agree) that implicit in this continuum is a place for any kind of fiduciary community Confucians might create.

Yet there is significance in what is not made explicit in the *Great Learning,* and what Tu somehow feels ought to be there. Needed to fill out the original idea for the modern mind is some intermediate stage between family and state, whereas for centuries the family had sufficed, it would seem, to provide the link between self and patriarchal state. I say, "it would seem," having in mind significant exceptions in more deeply thinking Neo-Confucians like Chu Hsi, Wang Yang-ming, Huang Tsung-hsi, Ku Yen-wu, and others who

worried about the lack of a significant infrastructure mediating between nuclear family and what had become a leviathan state. Chu
and Wang gave much thought to the importance of active community participation in the "community compacts" (hsiang-yüeh), and
Huang Tsung-hsi to the public roles of schools and academies.
Though little had come from or survived of these hopes by the
nineteenth century in China,[7] it is significant that in Korea the community compact associations, originally inspired by the writings of
Chu Hsi and his leading Korean interpreters,[8] served as the organizational base for popular political movements and uprisings in the
nineteenth century.[9] Other factors were obviously at work in the
latter case.

In China it is striking that our Neo-Confucian scholars, handicapped in performing their "prophetic" office by the lack of organized support among an articulate citizenry or from organs of
public opinion, all too often stood alone in facing the power con-
centrated in the ruler, or in coping with the Byzantine workings or
factional infighting of the imperial bureaucracy. The more conscientious of them could easily become martyrs, or more often political dreamers, but rarely successful statesmen achieving noble goals.
Thus, for Confucians as scholars in the late Ch'ing, it was natural
enough to look to the schools and academies (the way Fang Tung-
shu did) as the only sources of informed support, and for nineteenth-century reformers to turn to scholarly circles when, moved
perhaps by Fang Tung-shu's line of argument, they wished to mobilize public opinion through what was called ching-i, "pure (that
is, unvarnished) discussion." Yet the term "public discussion" could
be applied to this advocacy only in the sense of what was in the
common interest, conforming to Heaven's universal principles, not
in the Western sense of a "public" as a "people."

As Fang Tung-shu himself complained, the schools and academies themselves had long since ceased to serve as centers of public
discussion, which they had formerly done in the mid and late
Ming. And if, among religious or fraternal organizations, one still
might think to turn to secret societies (as rebels and revolutionaries
did), still their very secret or esoteric character ensured their mar-
ginality as organs of public advocacy.

Recent research by some historians of modern China has

pointed to signs that a local infrastructure, representing a "public sphere" roughly akin to "civil society" in Europe, began to appear in the late Ch'ing and early Republican periods (nineteenth and early twentieth centuries).[10] Here a distinction is made between the central government and its territorial agencies (referred to as *kuan*, the state bureaucracy), and a public sphere (*kung*) represented by a middle range of unofficial activities and organizations serving the general welfare or public interest, intermediate between the state and the common people (*min*). This new development is seen as tending to blur or bridge the traditional demarcation in Chinese society between ruling elite and subject masses.

Two aspects of these new studies on the "public sphere" are worthy of note. One is the increasing use of the word *kung* to describe voluntary activities undertaken in the general, common, or public interest. As a concept, *kung* was of course not new; it had appeared early in classical texts such as the "Evolution of Rites" of the *Record of Rites* in reference to what is shared in common, as well as in seventeenth-century writers like Huang Tsung-hsi and Lü Liu-liang, who deplored the failure of the dynastic state properly to serve the common or "public" interest. What is new in the more recent case is its application to extrabureaucratic endeavors on the part of local leaders who, as members of the educated elite, joined together in a public-spirited way to serve important social and philanthropic functions.

Some, at least, and perhaps much of the special currency gained by this term in published discourse is attributable to late-nineteenth-century writers influenced or challenged by contact with the West[11]—contacts that stimulated the rediscovery and reprinting of such works as Huang Tsung-hsi's *Ming-i tai-fang lu,* thereby linking the modern discourse to terms and texts which, though they were by no means unrepresentative of their own time or tradition, had largely disappeared from sight, or been actively repressed, under Ch'ing rule.

Another aspect of the problem is the actual activities or institutional developments to which the term *kung,* as representing a public sphere or public spirit, might be applied, either by the participants themselves or by later publicists. Enough research has now been done to document a significant increase in the level of volun-

tary, nongovernmental, and communal activities among the educated elite in both the waning years of the empire and the chaotic
decades of the early republican era.[12] Further, this activity sometimes led to the articulation of political demands going beyond the
local or provincial level—in other words, it suggests the incipient
formulation of public discourse on a national level (if we understand that "public" here refers to a concern for the general welfare
on the part of the elite, not to participation by commoners in general). To some extent this communal or collegial activism on the
intermediate level between state (*kuan*) and common people (*min*)
can be seen as prompted by—indeed almost induced by—the decline of central authority during and after the Taiping Rebellion, a
process only accelerated by the 1911 Revolution. In earlier periods
of dynastic decline, as in late Sung, Yüan, and Ming times, the
declining effectiveness of state administration and relaxation of central controls were attended by a similar rise in the number of voluntary associations for social, charitable, and scholarly purposes,
mostly on the local level but sometimes reaching up to the national.
As we have seen, when Fang Tung-shu in the 1840s called for a
revival of public discourse concerning critical national issues, he
cited the worthy example of learned public discourse (*chiang-hsüeh*)
in the late Ming academies, debating urgent national issues, and
even defended this independent activism against widespread
charges that the divisiveness of such debates had contributed to the
fall of the Ming.

To recall these historical parallels here or to suggest that the
more modern development of such an infrastructure may have
owed something to factors in a dynastic cycle or traditional pattern
of dynastic degeneration, is by no means to rule out the possibility
that new stirrings among the elite, potentially leading to significant
advances in the political order, may not also have been in the making. Further research may well demonstrate that, in the republican
period especially, promising possibilities did exist for the expansion
of a public domain going far beyond anything seen earlier.[13] Yet it
remains true, whether on account of the extreme deterioration of
the political and social fabric in these same years, or because of the
militaristic as well as the revolutionary and increasingly totalitarian
methods used to deal with this chaotic situation, the rather tender

growth, fragile character, and dispersed, fragmentary existence of this new infrastructure gave it little chance of survival amid the harsh struggles and intense repressions that ensued.

As a consequence, reform movements at the end of the dynasty and in the early republican period remained critically handicapped by the lack of an effective political base. Out of touch with the masses, unsupported by any party that could claim to be "popular" (that is, more than a faction), reformers were prophets without a people. Sun Yat-sen recognized this when he spoke of the Chinese as a "heap of loose sand" and sought, in the first of his People's Principles, to make them a people or nation in the Western sense. Yet, frustrated in his efforts to organize and effectively lead a revolutionary movement, Sun felt compelled to depart from his avowed democratic principles and, in desperation, adopt a doctrine of party tutelage, with strong authoritarian leadership as the only way to create national unity and democratic institutions. (As a one-party dictatorship of the Kuomintang, whose name had connotations of nationalism, populism, and democracy, Sun's doctrine of party tutelage could be taken, with hindsight, as an ominous foreshadowing of Mao's later "dictatorship of the people's democracy.")

Meanwhile, to the left of Sun, socialists and anarchists faced the same problem. Though their doctrines were predicated on a claim to represent the people or the proletariat, in fact, as Bertrand Russell noted in 1921, this remained, in the absence of any organization of people or workers, purely theoretical.[14] The collapse of the monarchy in 1911 had not altered this age-old condition.

After failure of the effort to create a "nation" through establishment of Confucianism as a state religion under Yüan Shih-k'ai's new monarchy in 1915–1916, and after years in which China was rent by civil war and foreign invasion, it was left to Mao Tse-tung to "go to the people," mobilize them politically, and organize them militarily in pursuit of revolutionary goals. At this point Mao linked up the prophetic tradition in the West, from which Marx emerged, and the Leninist conception of a revolutionary party, with the Chinese experience of peasant rebellion.

Unfortunately, having learned little from the long and conflicted Confucian experience, and understanding poorly the true depths and persistence of the troubles Confucians had run into, Mao underestimated the magnitude of the problem and made the historically unprecedented attempt, as revolutionary leader, of trying to combine in himself the roles of both prophet and sage-king. In the end, though Mencius' "people" exercised no right of revolution, they turned their backs on Mao and his retinue, leaving him too, like so many of his predecessors, a prophet without a people.

In the aftermath of the Cultural Revolution with its terrors and trauma—never, indeed, too well-hidden but now coming more and more to light—China's troubles are only too apparent. No less evident should be the determination of the Chinese to master them, the will to survive that has overcome so many past mistakes and misfortunes. Whatever its shortcomings, a cultural tradition symbolized by the phoenix, which has enabled the Chinese people to rise, again and again, above defeat and disaster, should not be underestimated. Whether China can catch up with the West by the year 2000, as the present leadership has vowed, may be doubtful, but already the Chinese people, though so far perhaps more abroad than at home, have shown themselves capable of taking the lead in many areas of modern life.

In this perspective there is no need to rush to final judgment. Earlier, when I wrote about "the liberal tradition in China," I wished simply to balance the record, to rectify the long-standing, lopsided view of Confucianism as wholly retrograde and reactionary, especially in its later stages. In showing that there was a more liberal side to Confucian tradition than had thus far been recognized, my aim was not to deny that this liberalism operated within very narrow limits or that the tradition also had its conservative side. In fact, no tradition could survive anywhere that was not to some degree both conservative and liberal—conservative of certain core values and liberal enough in adapting them to new circumstances and incorporating new ideas. It is only a modern revolutionary myth that sees such a long-lived tradition as all dead weight, standing stock still against the forces of history. Realism for us is to recognize historical change and seeming progress as multilinear and multiform, not to be gauged solely in relation to the West's directional course.

In the paroxysms of revolution, and especially in the May

Fourth movement of 1919, which, as the great breaking point between old and new, is celebrated as the highest expression of the liberationist spirit, Confucianism was made to stand for all that was backward and benighted in China. It bore all the burden of the past, charged with innumerable sins of the old order: political corruption and repression, the suppression of women, concubinage, female infanticide, illiteracy, etcetera, etcetera. Foot-binding was often cited as a prime symbol of a cramped, cruel, male-dominated Confucianism. In this the facts of history counted for little. It mattered not that, as to origins, foot-binding arose during the T'ang period, when Buddhism was dominant and Confucianism at a low ebb; nor, as to any association of ideas, did foot-binding have anything more to do with either Buddhism or Confucianism than whalebone corsets or spike-heeled shoes had to do with Christianity in the West. Except, be it noted for purposes more pertinent to our theme, that foot-binding, far from being a mark of subjection inflicted on the lower classes, represented a high fashion among the upper classes, and bespoke the extraordinary measure of sacrifice and self-discipline "noble women" might be expected to accept in order to "keep up," supposedly to maintain high standards in society.

Yet, should one pursue the thought, it might lead to the still more pertinent question: granted that Confucianism was not implicated in the adoption of such a practice, why did it not, in time, feel the need to criticize and oppose such practices as inhumane and essentially frivolous? Two thoughts occur. One is that this is not an unfair question to ask of a teaching so concerned with matters of good form—and of good form supposedly informed by a humane spirit. Another is that in the practice of concubinage and other customs demanding so much more forbearance and self-abnegation on the part of women than men, why did not the central principle of mutuality and reciprocity—said by the Confucians to be, along with loyalty and fidelity, the one thread running through all human relations—impose an equal burden on the husband as on the wife?

To the extent that rites had to do with basic forms of human respect, and as the highest formal expression of the ideals of the noble man even approximated "human rights," questions such as these would not be unreasonable ones to ask of any professed Confucian. But given the limits of the present inquiry, they must be left for some further and more balanced reassessment of the trouble with Confucianism, both in the light of history and in view of the modern critique of tradition. Of this the May Fourth movement, born out of extreme duress, was only the first anguished, and therefore understandably exaggerated and distorted, expression.

As to our main theme—the problematic relations of the ruler, the noble man, and the people—it takes no great expertise or insight to discern the persistence of the same difficulties in China today. The current leadership may be somewhat more enlightened and collegial in character than it was under Mao, but the political process has not yet been significantly broadened. Rule by a political elite, justifying itself as a party dictatorship ruling allegedly *for* the people (like the paternalistic dynasties of old), still tends to inhibit and repress the expression of popular opinion. No infrastructure has been developed which might exert a countervailing force. Indeed, by coming down hard on political activism in the universities and at T'ien-an men, the Party dictatorship has tended to insulate itself even from such "public opinion" as might be found there, in the absence of any other forum for open discussion and debate.

The implications of the T'ien-an men incident go beyond the obvious fact that a modern one-party state has instruments of control more coldly efficient than past dynasties. In the past, students and scholarly associations have been the natural vehicles for the expression of protest, and some at least of the student demonstration at T'ien-an men were conscious of reenacting a historic role— one which fell to them precisely because, as in the past, the state, in its need for trained personnel (even if not for liberally educated ones), could not do without schools. Temples and churches yes— these could easily be dispensed with or converted to other uses— but the prolonged closing of schools during the Cultural Revolution had dealt such a setback to modernization that anyone not blinded by Maoist ideology could see the damage being done to the state itself as well as society.

What students at T'ien-an men would have been less conscious of in their past, because the Stalinist curriculum imposed by Mao at the expense of the Chinese classics and any serious study of Chinese history allowed them little knowledge of it, was the tradition of Confucian protest against imperial despotism. Few of them would have known about Lü Liu-liang and Fang Tung-shu; a few more perhaps would have learned about the reformism of the Tung-lin school and Huang Tsung-hsi, but this reformism would have been dismissed as merely palliative—shoring up a rotten "feudal" system that should have been allowed to fall of its own dead weight. Likewise with the classic *Discourses of the States* and its account of the Duke of Shao protesting to King Li of Chou that his silencing of dissent among the people would only lead to a destructive outburst someday, like the devastating flood from a broken dam. Such ancient models as this would be known, if at all, only to a few specialists in early Chinese history or literature.

Against this background the dramatic appearance of the "Goddess of Democracy" at T'ien-an men takes on special significance. Whether inspired by the Statue of Liberty (a French creation) or by the classic female impersonation of "Liberté, Egalité et Fraternité," the Goddess was a symbol drawn from the French Revolution to become part of China's revolutionary inheritance from the West. It would have been associated by the young with the iconoclastic spirit of the May Fourth movement in 1919, and with the potent mythology of liberation so exploited by the Communists in the youthful days of their revolution. Least of all would it be identified with anything Chinese or with Confucian tradition.

It is hardly surprising then that the Teng regime, in its gerontocratic obsession with defense of the established order, would manage to treat the outpouring at T'ien-an men as a manifestation of subversive Western influences, and stake out a new claim—altogether at variance with its original liberationist ideology—that the protesters were unpatriotic, un-Chinese, irresponsible, and essentially anarchic.

A next step in this process of quarantining all protest as alien and illegitimate was a highly publicized and grandly promoted celebration of Confucius' birthday just weeks after the crackdown in T'ien-an men Square—indeed a celebration held just next door to the square itself. Of course nothing like this could take place without official approval and substantial logistical support, but neither the Party nor the government was a direct sponsor of the event. With this arrangement it was possible for earlier Maoist attacks on

Confucianism simply to go unmentioned; nothing need be retracted. Confucius, like Hitchcock's Harry, could reappear as if he had never been buried, and no one need feel haunted by his ghost as Mao had been.

The special nature of the event was manifested, however, when the leader of the Chinese Communist Party, Secretary General Jiang Zemin, made an unprecedented personal appearance. He spent two hours recollecting fondly his own Confucian upbringing, and gave his blessing to what was said by the chairman of the conference, Gu Mu, in his keynote speech. Since the latter speech was highly indicative of the government's likely long-term policy in cultural matters, the following excerpts are worth noting.

> The Chinese nation has had a long history and brilliant ancient culture. For a long period of time in human history, the Chinese culture, with the Confucian school of thought as the main stream, glittered with colorful splendor . . .
>
> Culture serves both as the emblem of the level of civilization of a nation or a country and the guidance for its political and economic life. To promote prosperity and peace for a nation and for mankind in general, it is necessary to develop a compatible culture. In this regard, a proper attitude toward the traditional national culture is very important. It is inadvisable either to be complacent about the past or to discard the past and the tradition. The correct attitude is to inherit the essence and discard the dross.
>
> The Chinese people are working hard to build socialist modernization and a prosperous and strong socialist country. In order to reach this goal, we must develop and improve our new culture, which, we believe, should be national, patriotic, scientific, and democratic. This calls for inheriting and reforming the traditional culture of our nation and parallel efforts to courageously and yet selectively assimilate the advanced cultures of the outside world, merging the two into an integral whole.
>
> As for the attitude toward the traditional culture and foreign cultures, there is no doubt that the traditional culture should be kept as the mainstay . . .
>
> As is known to all, the idea of harmony is an important component of the Chinese traditional culture. As early as in the last years of the West Zhou dynasty three thousand years ago, ancient scholars elucidated the brilliant idea of "harmony making prosperity."

Later, Confucius and the Confucian school put forward the prop-
osition of "harmony above all," and established theories on the co-
ordination of interpersonal relations, the protection of the natural
environment, and the maintenance of ecological balance. These
thoughts not only made positive contributions to the prosperity of
ancient Chinese society, but also have profound practical significance for the survival and development of mankind today.

In this marvelous cultural ballet, Gu Mu performs for several
audiences at once, domestic and foreign, and executes some grace-
ful ideological turns. Claiming the world-honored Confucius as
China's own, and Chinese culture as quintessentially Confucian, he
presents both Chinese tradition and the current regime as enlightened, progressive, and open to the world, while still relying on the
Confucian values of harmony and social discipline as the criteria for
excluding decadent libertarian influences from the West—screening
out the "spiritual pollution" already identified as responsible for the
alleged unbridled disorders of T'ien-an men.

From a strict Maoist point of view, there is nothing new in this
most recent attack on bourgeois liberalism as the alien virus infect-
ing rebellious Chinese intellectuals. Mao himself had urged Communist cadres to "combat liberalism" in the early rectification cam-
paigns of the revolution. What is different here, especially in
contrast to the Cultural Revolution's earlier vicious attacks on the
twin enemies of militant proletarian virtue, namely Confucianism
and bourgeois liberalism, is that now Confucianism, not Marxist
revolutionary morality, will guard the gates against Western deca-
dence. Meanwhile, niftily appropriated to Confucianism are the
Western liberal causes of environmentalism and ecology, which the
Communists had long before dismissed as specious imperialist pre-
texts for denying to undeveloped nations the benefits of industrialization.

To report this is not at all to assert that Confucianism has now
replaced Marxism-Leninism as the ideology of the one-party state.
For the present, Teng's policy still calls for the reaffirmation of
Communist orthodoxy and discipline. But the prevailing pragma-
tism of the modernization campaign in so many aspects of economic and cultural policy continues steadily to erode doctrinal orthodoxy; though the Party·can compel lip-service to time-worn

slogans, it cannot, by fiat, simply command assent or genuine commitment.

In this unfavorable climate, with much of the erstwhile Communist world (including the homelands of Marx, Engels, Lenin, and Stalin) having repudiated the original doctrine and practice of the Party, Beijing's pragmatic leaders will be disposed increasingly to lean on a conservative version of Chinese tradition as the best guarantor of the status quo. Since, moreover, such an inclination would follow in the direction of a growing trend among other conservative forces in East Asia, one can expect that the pragmatic Chinese leadership, rather than hold out as the last bastion of true Communist faith, along with Castro's Cuba, will find it more and more convenient to identify with Chinese tradition, conservatively interpreted, as a face-saving escape from a failed isolationism, looking now to a pseudo-Confucian tradition as its link to a new East Asian community.

Once more, then, Confucianism will be faced with its old predicament; its ancient trouble will be waiting for it again. Noble men and noble women, if any of either can still be found in post–Mao China, will confront the perennial dilemma: whether to repudiate, challenge, or make their peace with a state they themselves had not created, in hopes thereby of rescuing their people from a dire situation not of the Confucians' own making.

As one draws attention to these continuing problems of the Chinese, past and present, it would be invidious not to acknowledge that we in the West have similar problems of our own. True we do not lack for political advocacy, organs facilitating the expression of public opinion, or legal institutions to protect these. Yet how well we now make use of them in addressing the great challenges of our time—as urgent as any the Chinese, or Confucians in East Asia as a whole, faced in the nineteenth century—is another matter.

To ask this may seem odd at a time when we appear to be so well served by modern means of communication and mass education, and when the "public" would seem to be better informed than ever. But if the need is for more active learning and participation in meeting these challenges, while problems of intense urgency like those of the environment, drugs, poverty, education—so obvious that even to list them is a redundancy—go unmet year after year, we cannot claim to be doing much better than the Chinese of the nineteenth century who remained preoccupied with their own affairs, as if oblivious to the dangers threatening them. Going about their own Confucian business at least did not do great damage to other peoples, other species, the earth, and the heavens.

Can we say that today we are doing much better? Can we say that the modern television audience or other consumers of the mass media are any less passive and inert a people than China's peasant masses have been, or that even our television debates do substantially more than register certain charismatic personalities on the popular mind, without engendering much serious, reasoned discussion?

I do not raise these questions about the "public" as if the performance of scholars in the academy or teachers in higher education has been much better than that of the general public. Many of our leading research scholars contribute little or nothing to the discussion of urgent public questions, or even to the hard work of reexamining college curricula and redeveloping teaching methods to meet present needs. This is not, on the other hand, to associate myself with those who lament the lack of social consciousness on campuses today, and look back nostalgically to the activism of the sixties as heroic demonstrations of moral courage and social concern, before the dead hand of apathy set its cold grip on students in the late seventies and eighties. Radicals in the sixties, for their part, were rarely interested in promoting reasoned discussion; like the Cultural Revolutionaries of China, they sought simply to impose their own views and political will on others. Activists of that sort readily resorted to intimidation and bullying; often dissenting voices were shouted down or drowned out in the general clamor and disruption of serious discussion.

In such circumstances, then and still too often now, scholars and students run for cover, taking refuge in the idea that serious academic work at least contributes to the advancement of knowledge, even if one cannot bring it directly to bear on current issues. They have the same justification as the great classical scholars of the Ch'ing, whose monumental work still stands, but who were in a poor position to defend themselves against either the West or the penetrating critique of a scholar-prophet like Fang Tung-shu.

The Confucians paid a price for their stubborn adherence to a classical humanist tradition in the midst of a rapidly changing world, and were caught unprepared, as leaders in their society, to cope with the superior military and industrial power of the West. From the standpoint of "true" Confucians, however, who saw the essential problem as no less moral and spiritual than material, the real lapse lay not in the failure to industrialize and exploit more fully the earth's resources, but in the failure of an educational system too opportunistically oriented to career goals, and to careers narrowly defined in terms of office-holding in a dominant bureaucracy. Granted that not all of Chinese political culture was crass, self-serving, or short-sighted, yet even by traditional Confucian standards it had ceased to address fundamental human issues and new needs. Meanwhile the new learning from the West itself bypassed many of the same issues, and in the flush of momentary successes, failed to anticipate problems that would arise when there were no new worlds to conquer and no new lands to exploit.

These problems are no longer new, and our difficulty lies less in seeing them than in addressing them, less in advancing the frontiers of new knowledge than in arriving at a consensus on what values, what priorities, should guide our common efforts to remedy these problems. Educationally speaking, this focuses attention on the core curriculum, by which I mean a defined set of basic courses required of all students regardless of their field of specialization— courses that focus on the central problems of human life and society as revealed in pivotal works of the major world traditions, and that promote active civil discourse concerning the relevance of these core values to the problems of the contemporary world. This core, however, cannot be taken simply as a traditional given but must be seen rather as an arena of dialogue and discussion, in which the quality of the discussion will be as important as its outreach. On the one hand, no consensus on life-sustaining values can be arrived at without deep consideration of the traditional values that have so far sustained the human enterprise. On the other hand, a critical examination must be undertaken of past experience, and new directions must be found that would avoid past mistakes.

Today no people can look to their own traditions alone for this kind of learning and understanding, any more than could the Confucians earlier. The latter at least understood the need for dialogue and discussion as essential to "advancing in the Way," even though they were unable to sustain it, much less broaden it, in the given circumstances. Now the time has come for us to extend and expand the discourse, as a dialogue with the past, with other cultures, and even with future generations, who cannot speak for themselves but whose fate is in our hands.

Notes

Works Cited

Index

Notes

1. Sage-Kings and Prophets

1. *Shu Ching,* Yao tien. Tr. modified from Legge, *Chinese Classics* III, 1966, pp. 15–16.
2. *Shih ching,* Ta Ya, Wen Wang. Tr. modified from Legge, *Chinese Classics* IV, pp. 427–429.
3. David N. Keightley, "The Religious Commitment: Shang Theology and the Genesis of Chinese Political Culture," in *History of Religions* 17 (1978), pp. 211–225.
4. Hsü Cho-yün, *Western Chou Civilization,* New Haven: Yale University Press, 1988, pp. 146–147, 159, 163–171, 380.
5. *Shih Ching,* Ta Ya, Wen Wang. Tr. modified from Legge, *Chinese Classics* II, pp. 429–431.
6. The Chinese term is not specific as to gender, and in later times *chün* could be applied to women as well. Thus a reading like "noble person" is not impossible. But I think in patriarchal times "noble man" is closer to the actual meaning, and "person" should be reserved for *shen,* "one's own person," and the respect to which it is entitled.
7. The changed status and concept of the *chün-tzu* is discussed more fully in Hsü Cho-yün, *Ancient China in Transition,* Stanford: Stanford University Press, 1965, pp. 158–174.
8. Max Weber, *The Religion of China,* New York: Macmillan, 1965, pp. 227, 235.
9. Shmuel N. Eisenstadt, *This Worldly Transcendentalism and the Structuring of the World: Weber's Religion of China and the Format of Chinese History and Civilization,* Jerusalem: Hebrew University of Jerusalem, 1983.
10. Wm. Theodore de Bary, *Neo-Confucian Orthodoxy and the Learning of the Mind-and-Heart,* New York: Columbia University Press, 1981, p. 9.

11. Max Weber, *The Sociology of Religion,* Boston: Beacon Press, 1963, p. 46, as quoted by Peter Berger in "Charisma and Religious Innovation: The Social Location of Israelite Prophecy," *American Sociological Review* 28 (1963), p. 949.

12. Julia Ching, *Confucianism and Christianity,* Tokyo: Kodansha, 1977, p. 102.

13. D. C. Lau, Introduction to *Confucius: The Analects,* London: Penguin, 1979, p. 15.

14. John F. A. Sawyer, *Prophecy and the Prophets of the Old Testament,* Oxford: Oxford University Press, 1987.

15. Ibid., p. 22; the case is more fully elaborated in Berger, "Charisma and Religious Innovation," pp. 940–950.

16. Sawyer, *Prophecy and the Prophets of the Old Testament,* p. 22.

17. Ibid., p. 23.

18. D. L. Petersen, *The Roles of Israel's Prophets,* Sheffield: JSOT Press, 1981, p. 11, supports Sawyer's view when he says that "there is virtually no evidence to justify the claim that the prophets accumulated a following or exercised a leadership role." In most other respects the Confucians who play a prophetic role seem to fit Petersen's characterization of the "central morality prophet" as one who "legitimates or sanctions the central values and structures of the society and venerates a deity of distinct moral quality, a deity who is perceived as central to the social order" (p. 99). Heaven is so perceived by the Confucians, but can only be conceived as a "deity" with significant qualifications. Otherwise Petersen emphasizes that "the prophets performed their roles in different ways" (p. 98 and also 99). He does not go into the matter of the prophets' audience, except as they addressed the different societies of Judah and Israel. For purposes of assessing the potential transformative effect on society, however, the differences in Chinese society and the *chün-tzu*'s relationship to the people seem to me significant.

19. *Mencius* 6A:16.

20. *Mencius* 7B:34.

21. *Mencius* 7A:37.

22. D. C. Lau, *Mencius* VB:1, London: Penguin, 1970, pp. 149–150.

23. Weber, *The Sociology of Religion,* p. 46.

24. Abraham J. Heschel, *The Prophets,* New York: Harper, 1962, pp. 6, 14, 16.

25. Burton Watson, *Tso Chuan,* New York: Columbia University Press, 1988, p. xiv.

26. Ernest W. Nicholson, *God and His People: Covenant and Theology in the Old Testament,* Oxford: Clarendon Press, 1986, p. 201.

27. Ibid., p. 207.
28. Ibid., p. 208.
29. T. H. Robinson, *Prophecy and the Prophets in Ancient Israel,* London: Duckworth, 1923, 1979, pp. 69–70.
30. Nicholson, *God and His People,* p. 210.
31. Ibid., p. 215.

2. The Noble Man in the *Analects*

1. Nicholson, *God and His People,* pp. 201–215; Robinson, *Prophecy and the Prophets in Ancient Israel,* pp. 69–70.
2. Peterson, *The Roles of Israel's Prophets,* pp. 98–99.
3. Lau, *The Analects,* p. 85.
4. *Analects* 5:8, 5:19, 6:20, 6:22, 11:12, 14:1, 14:35.
5. *Analects* 15:32, 16:8, 18:6, 18:7.

3. Imperial Sages and Confucian Noble Men

1. *Shih Chi* PNP 6:23b; *Sources of Chinese Tradition* I, p. 141.
2. Ibid.
3. *Yen t'ieh lun,* sec. 19, 4:10b; *Sources of Chinese Tradition* I, p. 223.
4. Nashijima Sadao, "Butei no shi: Entetsuron no haikei," in *Kodaishi kōza,* Tokyo: Gakuseisha, 1965.
5. William Hung, *Tu Fu, China's Greatest Poet,* Cambridge, Mass.: Harvard University Press, 1952, p. 266.
6. Burton Watson, *Columbia Book of Chinese Poetry,* New York: Columbia University Press, 1986, p. 234.
7. Ting Ch'uan-ching, *Sung-jen i-shih hui-pien,* as translated in part by Chu Djang and Jane C. Djang, *A Compilation of Anecdotes of Sung Personalities,* New York: St. John's University Press, 1989, p. 400.
8. See Wm. Theodore de Bary, *The Message of the Mind in Neo-Confucianism,* New York: Columbia University Press, 1988.
9. See Wm. Theodore de Bary, *Neo-Confucian Orthodoxy and the Learning of the Mind-and-Heart,* New York: Columbia University Press, 1981, p. 158.
10. Ibid., p. 164.
11. This is a recurring theme in Ray Huang's *1587—A Year of No Significance,* New Haven: Yale University Press, 1981.
12. See Charles O. Hucker, *The Censorial System of Ming China,* Stanford: Stanford University Press, 1966, pp. 42–45. L. C. Goodrich and C. Y. Fang (eds.), *Dictionary of Ming Biography,* New York: Columbia University Press, 1976, pp. 308–311.

13. See Ja-Hyun Kim Haboush, "The Education of the Yi Crown Prince: A Study in Korean Pedagogy," in de Bary and Haboush (eds.), *The Rise of Neo-Confucianism in Korea,* New York: Columbia University Press, 1985.

14. Thomas A. Metzger, *Escape from Predicament: Neo-Confucianism and China's Evolving Political Culture,* New York: Columbia University Press, 1977.

15. As recorded in 1945 by Maeda Tamon, Minister of Education, who played an important role in drafting the rescript of January 1, 1946, whereby the Showa emperor renounced his divinity.

16. Wm. Theodore de Bary, *The Liberal Tradition in China,* Hong Kong: Chinese University Press, 1983, p. 84.

17. Lynn Struve, "Huang Zongxi in Context," *Journal of Asian Studies,* August 1988.

4. Autocracy and the Prophetic Message in Orthodox Neo-Confucianism

1. Robert Bellah, *Tokugawa Religion: The Values of Pre-Industrial Japan,* Glencoe: Free Press, 1957, pp. 196–197.

2. S. N. Eisenstadt, *This Worldly Transcendentalism and the Structuring of the World: Weber's Religion of China and the Format of Chinese History and Civilization,* Jerusalem: Hebrew University of Jerusalem, 1983, pp. 55–57, 66–70.

3. On Huang's critique of the Chinese dynastic state, see my discussion in *Sources of Chinese Tradition,* pp. 530–541 (pbk. edition), and my "Chinese Despotism and the Confucian Ideal," in J. K. Fairbank (ed.), *Chinese Thought and Institutions,* Chicago: University of Chicago Press, 1957, pp. 163–203.

4. *Ssu-shu chiang-i* (hereafter abbreviated SSCI), 1686 ed. of Ch'en Tsung, 29:10ab on *Chung-yung* 32.

5. SSCI 26:4a on *Chung-yung* 17.

6. SSCI 11:1ab on *Lun-yü* 8.

7. SSCI 3:13b on *Ta-hsüeh,* Chih-kuo, p'ing t'ien-hsia; *Ssu-shu Yü-lu,* T'ien-kai-lou ed. of 1684 (hereafter abbreviated *Yü-lu*), 4:10a.

8. SSCI 3:13b.

9. SSCI 3:14a; *Yü-lu* 4:10b.

10. SSCI 38:8ab on *Meng-tzu* 5a:6; *Yü-lu* 41:10ab.

11. SSCI 6:10ab on *Lun-yü* 3:19; *Yü-lu* 15:13b–14a.

12. SSCI 17:91 on *Lun-yü* 14:18; *Yü-lu* 26:21.

13. SSCI 37:1b–2a on *Meng-tzu* 4B:3; *Yü-lu* 40:2ab.

14. SSCI 6:10ab.
15. SSCI 29:2b on *Chung-yung* 27; *Yü-lu* 11:10b.
16. SSCI 29:10ab on *Chung-yung* 32; *Yü-lu* 12:6a.
17. Ch'iu Chün, *Ta-hsüeh yen-i pu*, Wen-yüan ko Ssu-k'u chüan-shu ed., 54:6a–7b. I owe this reference to Deborah Sommer.
18. SSCI 3:13b–14a on *Ta-hsüeh* 9, 10; *Yü-lu* 4:10ab.
19. See the earlier discussion of Huang Tsung-hsi in my *Liberal Tradition in China*, Hong Kong, Chinese University Press, 1983, p. 84.
20. SSCI 29:1b–2b on *Chung-yung* 27; *Yü-lu* 11:8ab.
21. SSCI 41:1ab on *Meng-tzu* 6B:1; *Yü-lu* 44:1ab.
22. SSCI 3:12a–13b on *Ta-hsüeh* 9: not in *Yü-lu*.
23. See Ch'ien Mu, *Hsin hsüeh-an*, pp. 107–122.
24. See *Sources of Chinese Tradition*, ch. 19, pp. 530–557.
25. SSCI 34:7b on *Meng-tzu* III A3; *Yü-lu* 37:16b–17a.
26. SSCI 24:4a on *Chung-yung* 1; *Yü-lu* 5:3b.
27. SSCI 1:19b on *Ta-hsüeh* 1; *Yü-lu* 1:25b.
28. *Yü-lu* 1:25b.
29. SSCI 1:19ab on *Ta-hsüeh* 1; *Yü-lu* 1:25a.
30. See Araki Kengo, *Yōmei-gaku no kaiten to Bukkyō*, Tokyo: Kembun shuppan, 1984, pp. 282–290. Jung Chao-tsu, "Lü Liu-liang chi ch'i ssu-hsiang," in *Fu-jen hsüeh-chih*, Dec. 1926, 5 (1–2), p. 35.
31. SSCI 29:1a on *Chung-yung* 27.
32. SSCI 34:10a on *Meng-tzu* 3A:3; Ch'ien Mu, pp. 80–81.
33. SSCI 29:1a.
34. Wm. Theodore de Bary, *East Asian Civilizations: A Dialogue in Five Stages*, Cambridge, Mass.: Harvard University Press, 1988, pp. 65–66.

5. Fang Tung-shu, a Prophetic Voice in the Early Modern Age

1. Liang Ch'i-ch'ao, *Ch'ing-tai hsüeh-shu kai-lun*. English translation published under the title *Intellectual Trends in the Ch'ing Period*, Immanuel Hsü (tr.), Cambridge, Mass.: Harvard University Press, 1959, p. 23.
2. Liang, *Intellectual Trends*, p. 78.
3. Hu Shih, *Tai Tung-yüan ti che-hsüeh*, Peking: Jen-jen wen-k'u, 1926, p. 175.
4. So characterized in Fang Chao-ying's biography of Fang Pao in Hummel, *Eminent Chinese*, p. 237. Fang Chao-ying was himself an excellent historian, and it was no particular prejudice of his but

rather the common assumption of his "emancipated" generation that he gave vent to in such an opinion.

5. As shown for instance in Fang's extensive critique of Huang Tsung-hsi's *Nan-lei wen-ting* (*T'ung-ch'eng Fang Chih-chih hsien-sheng ch'üan-chi*, Kuang-hsü ed., tse 42), or his discussion of Buddhism in *Hsiang-kuo wei-yen* (tse 34, 35, 36), as well as in the *Han-hsüeh shang-tui* itself.

6. Fang Tung-shu, *Han-hsüeh shang-tui*, Che-chiang shu-chu ed., 1840 (hereafter abbreviated *Shang-tui*).

7. *T'ung-ch'eng Fang Chih-chih hsien-sheng ch'üan-chi: K'ao-p'an chi wen-lu* (1948) 1:1a–13b (also in Morohashi Tetsuji et al., *Shushigaku taikei* [hereafter abbreviated SSGTK], Tokyo: Meitoku shuppansha, 1974, 11:430a) Pien-tao lun.

8. See the biographical and interpretive essay by Arita Kazuo in SSGTK 11, p. 36.

9. *K'ao p'an chi wen-lu* 4:31a–32b Chung p'ien Chang Yang-yüan hsien-sheng nien-p'u.

10. Ibid., p. 36.

11. SSGTK 11, p. 424a (282) Han-hsüeh shang-tui hou hsü.

12. *Shang-tui* 1:17b.

13. SSGTK 11, p. 424b (282) Han-hsüeh shang-tui hou hsü.

14. *Shang-tui* 1:20a–22b.

15. SSGTK 11, 424b (283) Hou hsü.

16. *Shang-tui* 1:15a–16b, 18ab.

17. *Ch'üan-chi*, tse 42, *Pa Nan-lei wen-ting* 30a–31a.

18. *T'ung-ch'eng Fang Chih-chih hsien-sheng ch'üan-chi, K'ao-p'an chi*, 1:1a–13b Pien tao lun.

19. *K'ao-p'an chi* 3:23b. Fang attributes this conception to Master Tung (*Tung Tzu*), but only the first sentence appears in the biography of Tung Chung-shu, *Han shu* 56 (Chung-hua ed. pp. 2518–19). The rest of the wording here I have been unable to locate in any of the extant writings of Tung or in the *Index du Tch'ouen Ts'ieou Fan Lou*, Peking: Centre Franco-Chinois d'études sinologiques, 1944, pp. 17–19, 94, 96–97. Wing-tsit Chan, in a personal communication, opines that the rest is Fang's own wording.

20. Ibid. 3:25a, 4:8a–10b, Ming-chi.

21. Fang underscores this in his preface to the *Han-hsüeh shang-tui*, 1b. As a major issue in Ch'ing thought, the subject is more fully dealt with in Benjamin Elman, *From Philosophy to Philology: Intellectual and Social Aspects of Change in Late Imperial China*, Cambridge, Mass.: Harvard University Press, 1984.

22. As excerpted in SSGTK 11:427a (291).

23. *Ch'üan-chi, K'ao-p'an chi* 4:32b–33b Fang Wang-chi hsien-sheng nien-p'u hsü.

24. So noted in the original editions of standard dictionaries such as *Tzu-hai* and *Tzu-yüan*.

25. *K'ao-p'an chi wen-lu* 4:32b–33b Fang Wang-chi hsien-sheng nien-p'u hsü. Also SSGTK 11:427ab.

26. *Shang-tui* 3:20b. For this fundamental aim of Chu Hsi, see my *Liberal Tradition*, pp. 21–24.

27. *Shang-tui* 3:21b–22a.

28. Ibid.

29. Ibid., 3:22a–23a.

30. Ibid., 3:25a.

31. Quoted by Burton Watson in *The Tso chuan*, New York: Columbia University Press, 1989, p. xv.

32. Ibid., 3:25ab.

33. *Lun-yü* 1:1.

34. *Shang-tui* 3:26a.

35. Ibid., 3:26a–27b. See also my *Liberal Tradition*, pp. 37–38. Fang also discusses the history of such discussion and the positive value of controversy as an essential element in scholarship and literature in a separate essay on Literary Debate found in *Ch'üan-chi, Shu lin yang chi* B:1a–7b Chu lin cheng-pien.

36. See Hamaguchi, "Hō Tō-shu no kangaku hihan ni tsuite," in *Nihon Chūgoku gakkaihō*, 30 (1978), p. 175a, citing the studies of Ōkubo Hideko in *Min-shin jidai shoin no kenkyū*, Tokyo: Kokusho kankō kai, 1976, p. 337.

37. The point is discussed in Hamaguchi, "Hō Tō-shu," pp. 170a–172b, and Elman, *From Philosophy to Philology*, pp. 242–245.

38. On the growing role of academies as research centers, see Elman, *From Philosophy to Philology*, pp. 136–137.

39. See my *Message of the Mind in Neo-Confucianism*, New York: Columbia University Press, 1989, pp. 208–216.

40. *K'ao-p'an chi wen-lu* 1:33b–40b, and *I-te ch'üan ying lu*, Hsia: 13b–14a.

41. *Shang-tui* 1: Chung hsü 3ab.

6. The Prophet and the People

1. Tsuchida Kenjirō, "Chen Hsiang's Thought and his Surroundings," in *Translations of the International Conference of Orientalists in Japan*,

22, 1987, pp. 116–118; and "Chin Jō no shisō to sono shūhen," in *Tōhōgaku*, 88, 1988, pp. 65–80. See also my *Liberal Tradition in China*, ch. 3.

2. *Journal of Asian Studies*, v. 46, no. 2, May 1987, p. 390.

3. Chang Po-hsing, *Cheng-i t'ang ch'üan-shu*, Fu-chou Cheng-i hsüeh-yüan ed. of 1868, 1:1, Personal preface to the *Ch'eng-shih jih-ch'eng*.

4. Chu Hsi, *Chung-yung chang-chü*, I.

5. Burton Watson (tr.), *Basic Works of Mo Tzu*, New York: Columbia University Press, 1963, p. 85.

6. See Tu Wei-ming, *Centrality and Commonality: An Essay on Confucian Religiousness*, Albany: Press of the State University of New York, 1988, ch. 5, pp. 115–116.

7. See my *Liberal Tradition in China*, pp. 32–35, 81–90.

8. See Sakai Tadao, "Yi Yulgok and the Community Compact," in de Bary and Haboush (eds.), *The Rise of Neo-Confucianism in Korea*, New York: Columbia University Press, 1985, pp. 323–348.

9. See An Pyong-uk, "The Growth of Popular Consciousness and the Popular Movement in the Nineteenth Century," *Korea Journal*, v. 28, no. 4, April 1988.

10. See William T. Rowe, "The Public Sphere in Modern China," *Modern China*, v. 16, no. 3, July 1990, pp. 309–329, for a review and appraisal of these recent studies.

11. See Hao Chang, *Liang Ch'i-ch'ao and Intellectual Transition in China*, Cambridge, Mass.: Harvard University Press, 1971; and I-fan Cheng, "*Kung* as an Ethos in late nineteenth century China: The case of Wang Hsien-ch'ien (1842–1918)," in Paul A. Cohen and John Schrecker (eds.), *Reform in Nineteenth-Century China*, Cambridge, Mass.: East Asian Research Center, 1976.

12. See Philip Kuhn, *Rebellion and Its Enemies in Late Imperial China: Militarization and Social Structure, 1796–1664*, Cambridge, Mass.: Harvard University Press, 1970; R. Keith Schoppa, *Chinese Elites and Political Change: Zhejiang Province in the Early Twentieth Century*, Cambridge, Mass.: Harvard University Press, 1982; and Mary B. Rankin, *Elite Activism and Political Transformation in China: Zhejiang Province, 1865–1911*, Stanford: Stanford University Press, 1986.

13. See David Strand, *"Civil Society" and "Public Sphere" in Modern China: A Perspective on Popular Movements in Beijing, 1919–1989*, Durham, North Carolina: Asian-Pacific Studies Institute, Duke University, 1990.

14. Bertrand Russell, *The Problem of China*, London: Allen and Unwin, 1922, pp. 169–170.

Works Cited

An Pyong-uk. "The Growth of Popular Consciousness and the Popular Movement in the Nineteenth Century." *Korea Journal*, v. 28, no. 4, April 1988.

Araki Kengo. *Yōmeigaku no kaiten to Bukkyō*. Tokyo: Kembun shuppan-sha, 1984.

Bellah, Robert. *Tokugawa Religion: The Values of Pre-Industrial Japan*. Geneva: The Free Press, 1957.

Berger, Peter. "Charisma and Religious Innovation: The Social Location of Israelite Prophecy," *American Sociological Review* 28 (1963), pp. 940–950.

Centre Franco-Chinois d'Etudes Sinologiques *Index du Tch'ouen Ts'ieou Fan Lou*. Peking: 1944.

Chang, Hao. *Liang Ch'i-ch'ao and Intellectual Transition in China*. Cambridge, Mass.: Harvard University Press, 1971.

Chang Po-hsing. *Cheng-i t'ang ch'üan-shu*. Fu-chou Cheng-i hsüeh-yüan, 1868.

Ch'eng, I-fan. "*Kung* as an Ethos in late nineteenth century China: The case of Wang Hsien-ch'ien (1842–1918)." In Paul A. Cohen and John Schrecker (eds.), *Reform in Nineteenth-Century China*. Cambridge, Mass.: East Asian Research Center, 1976.

Ch'ien Mu. *Chu Tzu hsin hsüeh-an*. Taipei: San-min shu-chü, 1971.

Ching, Julia. *Confucianism and Christianity*. Tokyo: Kodansha, 1977.

Ch'iu Chün. *Ta-hsüeh yen-i pu*. In Wen-yüan ko Ssu-k'u-ch'uan shu ed. Taipei: Taiwan Commercial Press, 1986.

Chu Hsi. *Chung-yung chang-chü*. In *Ssu-shu chi-chu*. Taipei: Chung-kuo tzu-hsüeh ming-chu chi-ch'eng, 1978.

Cohen, Paul A., and John Schrecker (eds). *Reform in Nineteenth-Century China*. Cambridge, Mass.: East Asian Research Center, 1976.

de Bary, Wm. Theodore. *East Asian Civilizations: A Dialogue in Five Stages*. Cambridge, Mass.: Harvard University Press, 1988.

———— *The Liberal Tradition in China*. Hong Kong: Chinese University Press, 1983.

———— *The Message of the Mind*. New York: Columbia University Press, 1988.

———— *Neo-Confucian Orthodoxy and the Learning of the Mind-and-Heart*. New York: Columbia University Press, 1981.

de Bary, Wm. Theodore; Chan, Wing-tsit; and Watson, Burton. *Sources of Chinese Tradition*. New York: Columbia University Press, 1966.

Dore, Ronald. *Taking Japan Seriously: A Confucian Perspective on Leading Economic Issues*. Stanford: Stanford University Press, 1987.

Eisenstadt, S. N. *This-Worldly Transcendentalism and the Structuring of the World: Weber's Religion of China and the Format of Chinese History and Civilization*. Jerusalem: Hebrew University of Jerusalem, 1983.

Elman, Benjamin. *From Philosophy to Philology: Intellectual and Social Aspects of Change in Late Imperial China*. Cambridge, Mass.: Harvard University Press, 1984.

Fairbank, John K. *Chinese Thought and Institutions*. Chicago: University of Chicago Press, 1958.

Fang Tung-shu. *Han-hsüeh shang-tui*. Hangchou: Che-chiang shu-chü, 1840.

———— *T'ung-ch'eng Fang Chih-chih hsien-sheng ch'üan-chi*. Kuang-hsü ed.

Greider, Jerome. "Review of Benjamin Elman's *From Philosophy to Philology.*" *Journal of Asian Studies*, v. 46, no. 2, May 1987.

Haboush, JaHyun Kim. "The Education of the Yi Crown Prince: A Study in Korean Pedagogy." In de Bary and Haboush (eds.), *The Rise of Neo-Confucianism in Korea*. New York: Columbia University Press, 1985.

Hamaguchi, Fujio. "Hō Tōshu no kangaku hihan ni tsuite." in *Nihon Chūgoku gakkai hō*, no. 30, 1978.

Heschel, Abraham J. *The Prophets*. New York: Harper, 1962.

Hsü Cho-Yün. *Ancient China in Transition*. Stanford: Stanford University Press, 1965.

———— *Western Chou Civilization*. New Haven: Yale University Press, 1988.

Huang, Ray. *1587—A Year of No Significance*. New Haven: Yale University Press, 1981.

Hucker, Charles O. *The Censorial System of Ming China*. Stanford: Stanford University Press, 1966.

Hummel, Arthur. *Eminent Chinese of the Ch'ing Period*. Washington, D.C.: Library of Congress, 1943.

Hung, William. *Tu Fu, China's Greatest Poet*. Cambridge, Mass.: Harvard University Press, 1952.

Hu Shih. *Tai Tung-yuan ti che-hsüeh*. Peking: Jen-jen wen-k'u, 1926.

Jung Chao-tsu. "Lü Liu-liang chi ch'i ssu-hsiang." In *Fu-jen hsüeh-chih*, Dec. 1926, 5 (1–2), pp. 1–86.

Keightley, David. "The Religious Commitment: Shang Theology and the Genesis of Chinese Political Culture." *History of Religions* 17 (1978), pp. 211–225.

Kuhn, Philip. *Rebellion and Its Enemies in Late Imperial China: Militarization and Social Structure, 1796–1864*. Cambridge, Mass.: Harvard University Press, 1970.

Lau, D. C. *Confucius: The Analects*. London: Penguin, 1979.

———— *Mencius*. London: Penguin, 1970.

Legge, James. *Shoo King*. In *The Chinese Classics*, v. 3, reprint of 2nd ed., Oxford University Press. Taipei: Wen-hsing shu-tien, 1966.

Liang Ch'i-ch'ao. *Intellectual Trends in the Ch'ing Period*. Tr. by Immanuel Hsü of *Ch'ing-tai hsüeh-shu kai-lun*. Cambridge, Mass.: Harvard University Press, 1959.

Lü Liu-liang. *Ssu-shu chiang-i*. 1686 ed. of Ch'en Tsung.

———— *Ssu-shu yü-lu*. T'ien-k'ai lou ed. of 1684.

Metzger, Thomas. *Escape from Predicament: Neo-Confucianism and Chinese Political Culture*. New York: Columbia University Press, 1977.

Morohashi Tetsuji et al. (eds). *Shushigaku taikei*. Tokyo: Meitoku shuppansha, 1974.

Nicholson, Ernest W. *God and His People: Covenant and Theology in the Old Testament*. Oxford: Clarendon Press, 1986.

Nishijima Sadao. "Butei no shi: Entetsuron no haikei." In *Kodaishi kenkyū*. Tokyo: Gakuseisha, 1965.

Ōkubo Hideko. *Min-shin jidai shoin no kenkyū*. Tokyo: Kokusho kankōkai, 1976.

Petersen, D. L. *The Roles of Israel's Prophets*. Sheffield: JSOT Press, 1981.

Rankin, Mary B. *Elite Activism and Political Transformation in China: Zhejiang Province, 1865–1911*. Stanford: Stanford University Press, 1986.

Robinson, T. H. *Prophecy and the Prophets of Ancient Israel*. London: Duckworth, 1923.

Rowe, William T. "The Public Sphere in Modern China." *Modern China*, v. 16, no. 3, July 1990.

Russell, Bertrand. *The Problem of China*. London: Allen and Unwin, 1922.

Sakai Tadao. "Yi Yulgok and the Community Compact." In de Bary and Haboush (eds). *The Rise of Neo-Confucianism in Korea*. New York: Columbia University Press, 1985.

Sawyer, F. A. *Prophecy and the Prophets of the Old Testament.* Oxford: Oxford Bible Series, Oxford University Press, 1987.

Schoppa, R. Keith. *Chinese Elites and Political Change: Zhejiang Province in the Early Twentieth Century.* Cambridge, Mass.: Harvard University Press, 1982.

Shu ching. In *Shih-san-ching chu-su.* Taipei: I-wen yin-shu-kuan, 1955. Reprint of 1815 ed. of *Sung-pen shih-san-ching chu-su fu chiao-k'an chi,* ed. Jüan Yüan.

Ssu-ma Ch'ien. *Shih chi.* In *Ssu-pu ts'ung-k'an,* Po-na-pen ed. Shanghai, 1930.

Strand, David. *"Civil Society" and "Public Sphere" in Modern China: A Perspective on Popular Movements in Beijing, 1919–1989.* Durham, North Carolina: Asian-Pacific Studies Institute, Duke University, 1990.

Struve, Lynn. "Huang Zongxi in Context." *Journal of Asian Studies,* August 1988.

Tsuchida Kenjirō. "Chen Hsiang's Thought and His Surroundings." In *Transactions of the International Conference of Orientalists in Japan. Tōhō-gaku* 22, 1987.

Tu Wei-ming. *Centrality and Commonality: An Essay on Confucian Religiousness.* Albany: Press of the State University of New York, 1988.

Watson, Burton (tr). *Basic Works of Mo Tzu.* New York: Columbia University Press, 1963.

—— *Columbia Book of Chinese Poetry.* New York: Columbia University Press, 1986.

—— *The Tso Chuan.* New York: Columbia University Press, 1989.

Weber, Max. *The Religion of China.* Tr. Hans Gerth. New York: MacMillan, 1965.

—— *The Sociology of Religion.* Boston: Beacon Press, 1963.

Index

The ancient
mind